WILL BRADLEY

His Graphic Art

A Collection of his POSTERS,
ILLUSTRATIONS, TYPOGRAPHIC
DESIGNS & DECORATIONS

Edited by

Clarence P. Hornung

DOVER PUBLICATIONS, INC., *New York*

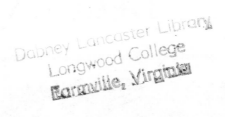
Published in Canada by General Publishing Company, Ltd., 30 Lesmill Road, Don Mills, Toronto, Ontario.
Published in the United Kingdom by Constable and Company, Ltd., 10 Orange Street, London WC 2.

Will Bradley: His Graphic Art is a new work, first published by Dover Publications, Inc., in 1974. Clarence P. Hornung made the selection of Will Bradley graphics (sources of individual works are given in the List of Plates); and Clarence P. Hornung and Roberta W. Wong wrote an introduction especially for the Dover edition. An autobiographical section (pp. xi-xxxi, "Notes Toward an Autobiography") was originally published in the booklet, *Will Bradley: His Chap Book*, The Typophiles, New York, 1955, copyright 1955 by Paul A. Bennett for the Typophiles, used by permission.

International Standard Book Numbers:
Clothbound edition: 0-486-22120-2
Paperbound edition: 0-486-20701-3
Library of Congress Catalog Card Number: 73-87711

Manufactured in the United States of America
Dover Publications, Inc.
180 Varick Street
New York, N.Y. 10014

Introduction to the Dover *Edition*

During the last years of the nineteenth century many respected artists turned to the creation of posters, pottery and glassware, elaborate needlework compositions and patterns for wallpapers and draperies. The current enthusiasm for handcraftsmanship and Art Nouveau, the style closely identified with the Arts and Crafts Movement, has encouraged many to turn to this earlier period, the 1890's, for artistic inspiration. Contemporary interest in the *fin de siècle* has led to the discovery of many artist-craftsmen whose work, out of favor for decades, has been neglected. Among those was Will Bradley, an American decorative illustrator and artisan who was esteemed in his own day as

> . . . a craftsman, in the best sense of this much-abused word; one who seeks to beautify the essentially utilitarian; one of that sturdy band of artists who, walking in the humble path of their own choosing, make the hardest kind of a fight against bad traditions and the prevailing custom and prejudices of mere commercialism; and one of those who succeed in giving the charm and dignity of art to objects of common use.

Born in Boston, Massachusetts, in 1868, Bradley was fascinated by type, printing, and illustration as a child. When he and his mother moved to Ishpeming, Michigan, after his father's death in 1879, he found a job as a printer's devil and later was foreman of the local newspaper. He composed with type at work, while in his spare time he earned extra money by designing posters. In 1886 he moved to Chicago to begin his career as an artist. He soon found his forte as a pen-and-ink illustrator, and by 1890 his work was appearing in *Frank Leslie's Illustrated Newspaper* and the Chicago trade journal, *The Inland Printer.*

Bradley did not have enough money to attend art classes during those early years in Chicago, and, instead, received his instruction from contemporary magazines, libraries, and local bibliophiles. Like many other self-taught artists of his day, he was quite aware of the latest developments in the art world, here and abroad. He must have read English and American essays on Japanese art and certainly observed how Eastern concepts of design were being assimilated into contemporary illustration and ornament. He studied British theories of art and decoration, such as those formulated by Owen Jones and Christopher Dresser. The Englishman who had the greatest impact upon Bradley and many of his contemporaries, however, was William Morris. Morris popularized the idea that the Arts and Crafts Movement had a mission. All the arts, from painting to furniture design, were to bring joy to the craftsman as he produced objects that, in turn, would make everyday life more beautiful. His firm, Morris and Company, a model for other craftsmen, created and sold wallpapers, fabrics, metalwork, furniture, and stained glass. Morris himself founded the Kelmscott Press, where he designed and printed many richly decorated books. The work of Morris and

his followers became identified with a particular style of design; decoration was derived from nature, but was simplified, usually symmetrical, and often interlaced with curving lines.

Bradley was also aware of another emerging English art movement that had originated from ideas proposed by Oscar Wilde. This school embraced no lofty moral tenets, but revered art for art's sake. The English school of design associated with this philosophy was related to an art movement that was developing on the Continent during the early 1890's; asymmetrical compositions, strong surface patterns, and dominating curvilinear rhythms were hallmarks of both British and Continental Art Nouveau.

In his early illustrations and ornaments, Bradley acknowledged his debt to the work of contemporary American draftsmen, to members of the English Arts and Crafts Movement (including Herbert Horne, Walter Crane, and William Morris), as well as his admiration for Japanese art. Although he realized a distinct sense of design by combining, as early as 1891, asymmetrical, curvilinear ornament with contrasting black and white areas, it was not until 1894 that his work dramatically matured into a thoroughgoing Art Nouveau style in a series of covers for *The Inland Printer* (Plates III,4,8,12,35,36,40) and several posters for a Chicago magazine, *The Chap-Book* (Plates I,IV,VIII,9,13). The catalyst, Aubrey Beardsley's illustrations for *Le Morte d'Arthur* and *Salomé*, inspired Bradley to achieve a new unity of design through increasingly expansive, curving lines and a subtle balance of bold, asymmetrical surface patterns and shapes. It would be most unnatural in a person so young and impressionable not to show evidence of numerous outside forces; at the same time, Bradley went beyond them and created something quite his own.

Bradley's posters and cover designs commissioned in 1894 marked the beginning of Art Nouveau in America, and along with the posters that Edward Penfield executed for *Harper's Magazine*, initiated the poster craze in this country. The work of countless Bradley imitators appeared at the newsstands, book stores, and on billboards, and provoked considerable comment from the startled, yet often enthusiastic public. Some who admired the poster as an art form marveled "at the growth and vitality of this class of design," while others, overwhelmed by the surfeit of placards, predicted its imminent demise. Bradley, who did not overestimate the importance of the poster as a new form, believed that it had a place in his role as an artist: "My constant efforts have been to make better and more refined that art which walks hand in hand with business."

His goal to beautify the utilitarian prompted him to leave Chicago at the end of 1894 for Springfield, Massachusetts. He planned to set up his own press, modeled after Morris's Kelmscott Press, where he could print advertising booklets and publish his own periodical. Much of his first year in Springfield, however, was spent completing commissions, including some of his finest Art Nouveau posters and covers for *The Chap-Book* (Plates 20,37), *The Chicago Sunday Tribune* (Plates 10,14), *The Echo* (Plate 15) and *Harper's Bazar* (Plates 21,24,29). Among his most outstanding commercial work from this period were his book illustrations, influenced by the black and white designs of Aubrey Beardsley, Charles Ricketts, and Laurence Housman. In Richard Blackmore's *Fringilla* (Plates 17-19), Bradley achieved a unity of type and illustration that prompted a critic for *The Book Buyer* to see Bradley as "the pioneer . . . the head of an American movement, similar to that which is taking place in England, France, and Germany, toward beautiful artistic books."

Shortly after *Fringilla* was published Bradley established the Wayside Press and by May 1896, the first issue of *Bradley: His Book* appeared at the newsstands (prospectus, Plate 27). An art and literary magazine like many of the bibelots which proliferated during the 1890's, *Bradley: His Book* was distinguished by the outstanding decorative illustrations that enriched the text and advertisements (Plates 30-34, 41-47). Bradley himself wrote several short stories for the magazine, again following the example set by William Morris, who once said, "If a chap can't compose an epic poem while he's weaving tapestry he had better shut up; he'll never do any good at all." As *Bradley: His Book* became both a critical and financial success, Bradley was encouraged to sponsor his own arts and crafts movement by promoting in his magazine good art and design in the gallery, the book, the advertisement and the home. He planned to report on the latest developments in the fine arts . . . and "Architecture, with special reference to the planning of interiors. . . ." The graphic arts were to be represented by the discussion of "Book Illustration, in all its new developments. . . ." He considered applied art, decoration and design for the home to be part of the crafts revival, and planned to include articles on embroidery and china painting, and "suggestions for the artistic arrangement of the home, and designs for screens, portieres, settles, cozy-corners, window-seats, etc." To guide the amateur he promised to provide "full-sized working patterns of novel and pleasing designs" (Plates 60-61). In his Springfield studio he also intended to produce "pictures, books, tapestries, and artistic effects generally," along with "wallpapers and all kinds of mural decorations, including fabrics."

Although many of these plans were never realized, the Wayside Press produced much outstanding work from 1896 until 1898. Bradley arranged, illustrated, and printed numerous books for his own sale and for such publishers as Way and Williams and the English firm, John Lane. Advertisements printed at the Wayside Press were recognized by trade journals as important and influential examples of commercial design. Bradley, however, exerted his greatest influence on the printing world. Throughout his life he had been intrigued by type: as early as 1891 he had designed several type faces for *The Inland Printer,* and in 1895 the American Type Founders bought the rights to the lettering he created for one of his *Inland Printer* covers (Plate 35). Bradley drew upon his study of colonial American and eighteenth-century English printing and introduced in his work at the Wayside Press, Caslon Roman and italic type, which he combined with woodcut initials and ornaments. The trade journals quickly adopted this scheme, and one critic observed,

> . . . there is no mistaking the immediate importance and value of Mr. Bradley's work. It is bound to have an enormous influence upon all printing of the future. His aims and efforts are as far above those of the established printing trade as were the aims and ideals of William Morris. . . .

A critical success, the Wayside Press was disbanded at the end of 1898 when Bradley found his health threatened by the demands of his job. He sold his press to the University Press at Cambridge, Massachusetts, and went to work for this firm to help meet his financial obligations. For the next two years he continued to arrange and illustrate brochures and books, and brought the same kind of acclaim to his new employer that had once been showered upon his own press.

Toward the end of his tenure at the Cambridge firm he began to accept freelance commissions. In 1899 he designed a new layout for *The Bookman* and *Harper's Weekly,* and at the turn of the century, he was asked to arrange a new editorial prospectus for *The Ladies' Home Journal.* Although this project was never executed it did introduce Bradley to the editor, Edward Bok, who commissioned the artist, after

he had left the University Press, to create for the *Journal* a series of home interiors to be called "The Bradley House" (Plates 78–79). His continuing interest in the English Arts and Crafts Movement was apparent in these designs where the pictorial, elegant and whimsically imaginative qualities of his work often set Bradley apart from his American contemporaries Frank Lloyd Wright and Gustav Stickley and linked him more closely to the English craftsmen and architects M. H. Baillie Scott and C. F. A. Voysey.

During this period Bradley resumed his career as an illustrator, and in 1900 and 1901 he completed a series of covers for *Collier's Magazine* (Plates 72,75,81,86). These and the illustrations which he designed for the two children's stories that he wrote, "Castle Perilous" and *Peter Poodle, Toymaker to the King* (Plates 58,85), reveal dramatic changes in his drawing style. Gone are the rhythmical Art Nouveau curves, the dramatic, asymmetrical juxtaposition of patterns, replaced by more static and contained compositions. Although in much of his late work Bradley reflected a trend in American illustration toward the pictorial by introducing three-dimensionality and modeling into his *Collier's* covers, he continued to emphasize the decorative qualities of each design through strong contour outlines and symmetrical compositions, and like Maxfield Parrish preferred ornamental frontal and profile caricature figures. After the turn of the century Bradley also continued to draw his woodcut ornaments, a bold and angular style that had interested him since his Wayside Press days.

Another commission from this period was an advertising campaign that he undertook for the American Type Founders. For this firm in 1904 and 1905 Bradley wrote, arranged, and illustrated a series of twelve monthly magazines, *The American Chap-Book.* In these little booklets Bradley continued to espouse the cause which had concerned him most of his career, to merge art with business, by advising businessmen how to design effective advertisements with American Type Founders type and ornaments (Plate 84). Once again the critics received Bradley's work with praise: "It is safe to predict that this is really a remarkable little publication and will in the future take its proper place as a distinct contribution to the subject of good typography." It is interesting to note that Bradley was still studying the work of his English contemporaries. One of the series of ornaments which Bradley designed and introduced in *The American Chap-Book*, the Chap-Book Cuts (used as decorations in the introduction and autobiographical pages of the present edition), were partially derived from woodcuts devised by Joseph Crawhall in the late 1880's.

Bradley's interest in type design and layout, encouraged by his work for the American Type Founders, demanded more and more of his attention, and by 1907, when he became art editor of *Collier's Magazine*, his career as an artist essentially had come to a close. From 1910–1915 he was simultaneously art editor of *Good Housekeeping, Metropolitan, Success, Pearson's,* and *National Post.* In 1915 he was art supervisor for a series of motion pictures financed by William Randolph Hearst, and from 1918 to 1920 he wrote and directed his own picture, *Moongold.* During the 1920's he was back working for Hearst as art supervisor for all his publications. This busy career left little time for his own art work. Although Bradley ran an art service in New York from 1912–1914, and wrote and illustrated another children's story, *Wonderbox Stories,* in 1916 (Plate 88), this work could not match the originality of the designs of his youth; instead, he had chosen to direct his energy and creativity to the printing world, to bring gaiety and life to the printed page.

By the time Art Nouveau was being rediscovered by the present generation, and arts and crafts had become a fashionable pursuit, Bradley himself was scarcely aware of his early achievements. He was somewhat surprised by the recognition he received during the 1950's until his death in 1962. In California the Rounce and Coffin Club commended his fine work as a printer and draftsman and the Huntington Library presented an exhibition of his illustrations, books, advertisements, and typography. The American Type Founders honored their long-standing association by commissioning Bradley to design a series of type ornaments, while Strathmore Papers, one of his first customers at the Wayside Press, asked him to decorate a selection of paper samples for an advertising campaign.

In 1955 the Typophiles published a little book of Bradley's reminiscences that capture the enthusiasm and energy of this innovative illustrator and printer. This brief autobiography is reprinted in its entirety in this Dover edition. Bradley's memory for dates is inexact at some points, and the material alternates between second and third person because it was originally compiled from various sources. It furnishes, however, a completely delightful introduction both to Will Bradley and to his times.

Sources for the various graphics are shown in the List of Plates. The order of presentation of the material is, wherever possible, chronological.

It is the fervent hope of the publishers and the undersigned that this void in documenting Will Bradley's talents and versatility will be filled, in some small measure, by the present volume. At the same time, the editors express their grateful thanks to the New York Public Library, the Metropolitan Museum of Art, and various friends of Mr. Bradley's for their help in assembling the examples shown herein. The editors are particularly indebted to Mrs. Fern Bradley Dufner of La Jolla, California, Will Bradley's daughter, whose gracious cooperation helped make this book possible.

CLARENCE P. HORNUNG
ROBERTA W. WONG

New York 1973

Will Bradley: Notes Toward an Autobiography

THE BOY PRINTER OF ISHPEMING

It is graduation day in the little brown schoolhouse on Baltimore Street in Lynn, Massachusetts, just outside Boston. Miss Parrot is the teacher—a dear! You are six years old; next month you will be seven. The blackboard is covered with chalk drawings: sailboats, steamboats, ferryboats, trains of cars, houses, people and animals. You are the artist. Your mamma, with other mammas, is sitting on the platform, proud of her Willie—who is probably plenty proud of himself.

Lynn is a shoe town. This is 1875. Most of the work is done by hand. The employees are all natives—Universalists and Unitarians, probably. Many women work at home, binding uppers and tongues of high, lace shoes. You have a little express wagon. You carry finished work back to the factories and return with a supply of unfinished. For each trip you are paid five cents. With your savings you buy a printing press. It is the kind you place on a table and slap with the palm of your hand. In business offices it is used to stamp date lines. Your father is drawing cartoons for a Lynn daily—perhaps the *Daily Item*. He brings you a box of pi. When you succeed in finding a few letters of the same font you file them to fit the type slot in the press.

Your father is ill, an aftermath of the Civil War. You have moved to the section called Swampscott. This is too far away for you to attend the school to which your class has gone. Your mother goes out every day to do dress-making. A playmate takes you to his school. But most of the time you remain at home with your father. He tells you he hasn't long to live, says you have been a good boy and that when you grow up you will want to be an artist and there will be no money for your education. He gives you much fine advice which you never forget. Then he sends you out to play. You go to Fisherman's Beach and watch the fishermen take lobsters out of the boiling pot. They give you the little ones the law forbids selling. You crack them on a rock, and have a feast. Sunday mornings, or occasionally on a Saturday night, you go to the baker's and get your warm pot of baked beans and buy a loaf of brown-bread—always an event of delicious anticipation. Between meals, when you are hungry, there is often a cold cod-fish cake to be found in the pantry.

Your mother and you are now alone in the world and you are on the "Narrow Gauge" on your way to Boston. You are sucking a "picklelime," always found in glass jars at the candy counter of every railroad and ferry waiting room. It will be made to last until you reach Boston and are at the Park Street corner of the Common watching the Punch and Judy show while your mother is shopping. At noon you sit in a booth and eat clam chowder at a restaurant on Corn Hill. After the meal your mother takes you to a wholesale house where she has a friend. Here you are bought a suit of clothes.

"But isn't it too big, Mamma?"

"Yes, dear; but children grow very fast and soon it will fit you—and Mamma can't afford to buy you a new suit every year."

And now you are on your way to Northern Michigan, where your mother has a sister whose husband is paymaster at the Lake Superior Iron Mine. En route you stop at Providence where you are intrigued by the teams of twenty or more horses that pull freight cars through the down-town districts. You think it would be fine to be a teamster. At Thompsonville, Connecticut, you go to school for a few weeks. On circus day you are allowed to have a vacation. You ride a pony in the parade and ask your mother if you can't join the circus and ride in the parades every day.

It is your first day in the little mining town of Ishpeming. You are standing in the middle of the road watching children going home from school; the girls giggle, the boys laugh at the new boy in a too-big suit. One little girl has cute pigtails. You like her. You are now quite grown up, nearly ten. At a Sunday-school picnic you tell the little girl you are someday going back to Boston and learn to be an artist. You ask her to wait for you. She promises. With this important problem settled you can now give all of your attention to the question of how you are to get an art education.

In the fall you go to school and somehow manage to pull through. Your uncle and aunt go for a visit "back East." Your mother keeps house for your cousins. Every night when you go to bed you kneel down and ask God to tell your uncle to bring you a printing press, the kind with a lever, like the ones shown in the *Youth's Companion.* Your uncle brings you an Ingersoll dollar watch.

It is your second year in school. You now have a step-father. He is a fine man and you like him and he likes you—but of course you can't expect him to pay for your art education. You are having trouble with arithmetic—something in division. Teacher says, "Take your books and go home, Willie, and remain until you have the correct answer."

You don't like arithmetic, anyway.

"Mother," you ask, "may I go to work and earn money so I can learn to be an artist?"

Your mother is troubled. Finally she says, "Perhaps it will be for the best."

You go to the office of the *Iron Agitator,* that later became *Iron Ore.* George A. Newett is the owner and editor. This is the George A. Newett and the newspaper that were later sued for libel by Theodore Roosevelt. The trial took place in Marquette, Michigan, and Mr. Roosevelt won a verdict of six cents.

You are put to work washing-up a Gordon press. Then you receive your first

Newspaper masthead 1886

lesson in feeding. There is power, a small engine mounted on an upright boiler, for the newspaper press. The two jobbers are kicked. Having half an hour of leisure you learn the lay of a lower-case beside the window—where you can proudly wave to the schoolchildren as they are going home to their noon meal. You are now a working man—wages three dollars a week.

Country newspaper shops train and use local help for straight matter. For job work, ads and presswork they depend upon itinerant job printers, who seldom remain as long as six months in any one town. When the *Iron Ore* job printer leaves you are sorry. He has been a kind and patient teacher. You are now twelve. Mr. Newett employs a new devil and you set jobs, advertising display, make up the paper and are responsible for all presswork. Your wages are increased to six dollars a week. When the motor power fails, as it does frequently, you go out on the street and employ off-shift miners to operate the press by means of a crank attached to the flywheel.

At this early date the print shop is above a saloon and in one corner of a big barn of a room that had been a lodge hall. In winter it is heated(?) with one stove. You go to work at seven and quit at six. The outside temperature is below zero. You and your devil forage in the snowdrifts of the alley back of the building and "borrow" packing boxes to get kindling for the stove and boiler.

The *Peninsula Record*, across the street, is a four-page tabloid. It is printed one page at a time on a large Gordon. The owner and editor is John D. West. He offers you eight dollars a week. You are not that important to Mr. Newett—and the extra two dollars will enable you to begin saving after paying board and buying your clothes.

In a few months *Iron Ore* moves into a new store-building. You are now thirteen and Mr. Newett offers you ten dollars a week and the acknowledged position of job printer. At fourteen this wage is increased to twelve. At fifteen you are spoken of as foreman and are receiving fifteen dollars a week—in '85 a man's wages.

This is the early Eighties. Small towns such as Ishpeming are "easy pickings" for traveling fakers. Their advance is always heralded by the exchanges. They clean up at the expense of local merchants. All editors warn them to keep away. *Iron Ore* print shop is on the ground floor. The editor's sanctum is at the front. His desk is at the big window. It is nearly nine o'clock on a Friday night—"makeup" time. Mr. Newett has written his last sheets of copy and is reading proof. At the corner of Main and Division, diagonally across from the office, a faker is selling soap. In one wrapper he pretends to place a five dollar bill—a version of the "old army game." He is standing in a market wagon and has a companion who strums a guitar and sings. Attached to an upright and above his head is a kerosene flare. Mr. Newett walks leisurely to where there are several guns and fishing rods in a corner. He is an inveterate sportsman in a land where game, deer and fish, is plentiful. Selecting a rifle he walks to the door and casually puts a bullet through the kerosene tank, then returns to his proof reading. Thoroughly likable, this pioneer editor—a fine boss, a true friend!

You and a compositor now have control of the town bill posting. When there are no theater or patent medicine ads to put up you cover the boards with blank newsprint and letter and picture advertisements for the stores.

You are sixteen, almost seventeen. A sheet of newsprint is tacked on the printing-office wall and, using marking ink and a brush, you are picturing and lettering a masquerade poster for the roller rink.

"Who is this young artist?"

The speaker is Frank Bromley, a well-known landscape painter from Chicago.

You tell him about your father and that you are going back to Boston to study art. He suggests your stopping off in Chicago to see him. Says he can perhaps help you.

You are nearly seventeen and already you have saved more than fifty dollars. By the early fall you have four twenty-dollar gold pieces under your socks in the top till of your trunk. Wages are always paid in gold and silver. You are now ready to start for Chicago. Two weeks later you are on your way.

FIRST SOJOURN IN CHICAGO

The artist has a studio near the McVickar Theater on Madison Street. It is the typical atelier of the Victorian Eighties: oriental drapes, screens and pottery. Jules Guerin, then an art student and later a contributor to *Century*, *Harper's* and *Scribner's*, is clearing up and tidying for the day.

Mr. Bromley takes you to Lyon & Healy. Yes, Mr. Lyon, or maybe it was Mr. Healy, can start you as an apprentice. However, a young man beginning a career should be most careful in making his selection. You have been careful. You want to be an artist. But the business of Lyon & Healy is musical instruments, not art.

Next morning you are introduced to Mr. Rand, or Mr. McNally. A Mr. Martin then sends you upstairs, a couple of flights, to Mr. Robinson in the designing and engraving department. Beginners do not receive any pay, but you are put to work at a long table facing a row of windows and with yards and yards of unbleached cotton-cloth stretched on a wire at your back. You are now learning to engrave tints on wood-blocks—under the erroneous impression that designers and illustrators engrave their own blocks.

Mr. Bromley has found a room for you at the home of a friend, an art dealer. It is at Vincennes Avenue and Fifty-ninth Street. You walk to and from Rand McNally's, located on Monroe Street, dreaming happily.

One morning, after a few weeks of getting nowhere, for you are no master of tint-cutting, it percolates through your skull that inasmuch as wood-engravers never seem to be doing any designing probably designers never do any engraving.

A momentous discovery, this, for you have broken into your last twenty-dollar gold piece—as a matter of fact there is just about enough left to pay for taking your trunk to the depot and to buy a second-class ticket back to that printing shop in Northern Michigan.

"Sometime, if you care to come back," states Mr. Robinson, in a letter which must have been written immediately after your departure, "and if you will remain half an hour later in the evening and sweep out, and come in a half hour earlier in the morning and dust, Rand McNally will pay you three dollars a week."

SECOND SOJOURN IN CHICAGO

A few months later, when you have just turned into your eighteenth year and have saved sixty dollars, three twenty-dollar gold pieces, it is time to return to Chicago. You tell Mr. Newett. He wishes you well and says that if you care to remain with *Iron Ore* he will take you into partnership when you are twenty. This is a big temptation. You admire and like your boss. He is a grand person—your idol. Saying goodbye involves a wrench.

You are now back with R-M staying half an hour at night and getting to work a half hour earlier in the morning and all is well with the world.

At the time of your first visit to Chicago, line photo-engraving was not even a whisper, and halftones were not even dreams. On your second visit, pen drawings are beginning to receive direct reproduction.

Folding machines are unknown; and in a large loft, at long tables, dozens upon dozens of girls are hand-folding railroad timetables. This loft is on a level with the designing department. Between the two there is a brick wall through which, about two feet up from the floor, has been cut an opening in which there is a heavy, tin-covered sliding door. When you take 14 x 22 metal plates down to the foundry to be routed—by someone else, for you don't like machines—you pass through this loft, between the girl-adorned tables. You, in turn, are adorned with the side-whiskers known as mutton-chops—trying to look older than your years. Also, in accord with the custom of the times, you wear tight-fitting pants. One day, in returning from the foundry with a metal plate on your shoulder, you pull back the sliding door and when you lift one leg to step through the opening the pants rip where the cloth is tightest. On another occasion when again carrying a plate on your shoulder your jacket pocket catches on a key at the end of a paper-cutter shaft and the shoddy that had once proved so disastrous in your pants now probably averts a serious accident.

Web presses and automatic feeders are also absent. In the basement at Rand McNally's there is a battery of drum-cylinders printing James S. Kirk "American Family Soap" wrappers. The stock is thin, red-glazed paper, and the sheets a double 24 x 36, or perhaps even larger. You marvel at the skill with which boys do the feeding; but even greater is your wonder at the hand-jogging and cutting of these slippery and flimsy sheets.

Invitations are sent out for an inspection of the composing-room of the *Chicago Herald,* now newly equipped throughout with Hamilton labor-saving furniture. You attend. Compositors are sticking type for the next edition. A little later the *Herald* places on display its first web press. This showing is in a ground-floor room, a step or two down from the street, next door to the Chicago Opera House, where Kiralfy's *Black Crook* is now playing and Eddie Foy is putting audiences in "stitches." The press is a single unit standing in a shallow pit surrounded by a brass rail.

Comes now the winter. It is a Saturday. You are at the home of your boss. He has invited you to spend the afternoon learning how to paint. His easel is set up in the basement dining room. He is talking to you about religion, gravely concerned at learning that you sometimes attend the Universalist church. He believes you to be a heathen and suggests that you become converted and join a fundamentalist church—says that as long as you remain outside the fold and thus are not a Christian he cannot be interested in helping you become an artist.

The dear man! He wants so much to save your soul. Meanwhile, his good wife is laying the table for their evening meal. Her smile is motherly. Maybe she has guessed you were counting the plates. Pleasant odors come from the kitchen. Our gracious host brings your coat, helps you put it on, hands you your hat, opens the door and you step out into a Chicago snowstorm.

At this point the script calls for slow music and heart-rending sobs—another Kate Claxton in the *Two Orphans.* Alas for melodrama! This is a beautiful snowstorm. The evening is mild and the flakes are big. They sail lazily through the amber light of the street lamps, feather the bare branches of trees that print a fantastic pat-

tern against the red-brick housefronts. The drifts must be at least an inch deep. And tomorrow . . . tomorrow, you will, as always happens on Sunday, go to a restaurant on Clark Street where you will be served two pork tenderloins, flanked by a mound of mashed potatoes topped with gravy, and one other vegetable, and supplemented by bread and butter and a cup of coffee—all for twenty cents. Joy bells ringing!

A couple of weeks later you are standing at a case in the printing plant of Knight & Leonard. Mr. Leonard happens to be passing. He stops and glances at your galley, type arrangement for a catalog cover. He is interested and asks where you learned job composition. In one graphically condensed paragraph, dramatically composed, for it has been prepared in advance in anticipation of this much wished-for opportunity, you tell the story of your life—and make a momentous proposition.

The next morning you are seated at a flat-top desk in the second-floor office. You have your drawing material and are designing a new booklet cover for the stationery department of A. C. McClurg. It is understood that when orders for drawing fail you will fill in by setting type.

Now you are, at nineteen, a full-fledged designer and working at a window opposite Spalding's. On playing days you watch Pop Anson and his be-whiskered team enter a barge and depart for the ball park.

One day a young man appears at K & L's with proofs of halftone engravings. He has been with the Mathews Northrup Press in Buffalo, where he had learned the process. He is now starting an engraving plant in Chicago. K & L print some specimen sheets on coated paper. These are probably the first halftones ever engraved in Chicago, also the first printing of halftones. K & L are Chicago's leading commercial printers, quality considered. Mr. Knight is a retired Board of Trade operator. Mr. Leonard is the practical printer. He is also the father of Lillian Russell. Once, when she is appearing in Chicago, Miss Russell visits at the office. You are thrilled.

A man, trained in Germany, grinds ink for K & L. He is located on the floor above the office. You occasionally visit him. He gives you much good advice. The *Inter Ocean*, located on the next corner, installs a color press. The K & L ink expert helps get out the first edition.

For two years or more you occupy that desk and never again see the composing room. During this period, while receiving twenty-four dollars a week, you marry that young lady of your ten-year-old romance.

The J. M. W. Jeffery Co., show printers, is turning out some swell posters designed by Will Crane. They are printed from wood-blocks and are wonders. An artist by the name of Frank Getty is designing labels in the Chicago sales-office of the Crump Label Company. They are a glorious departure from the conventional truck of the label lithographers.

Joe Lyendecker is designing covers in color for paper-bound novels. They are gorgeous. There are no art magazines or other publications helpful to designers. You, like others, have a scrap-book made up of booklet covers, cards and other forms of advertising. A designer by the name of Bridwell is doing some thrilling work for Mathews Northrup in Buffalo, a concern that is setting a stiff pace for other railroad printers. Abbey, Parsons, Smedley, Frost and Pennell, and Charles Graham in *Harper's Weekly*, are models for all illustrators.

You are now free-lancing and making designs for Mr. Kasten of the McClurg stationery department. You have a studio in the new Caxton building on Dearborn

Street. You work all of one day and night and part of the next day on some drawings
for Mr. Kasten. He comes to get them at four o'clock on the afternoon before Christmas. You tell him you haven't eaten since the previous night.

He takes you and your drawings in a cab and stops at a saloon in the McVickar
Theater building and buys you an egg nog. "Drink this," he says. "It will put you on
your feet until you reach home and can get dinner." It is only a glass of milk and egg
—and looks harmless. You get on the Madison Street horse-car, and take a seat up
front. There is straw on the floor to keep your feet warm. You promptly go to sleep.
The car bumps across some tracks and you wake long enough to know your stop is
only two blocks away. In getting off the car the straw tangles your feet and you seem
to be falling over everyone. The sidewalk is not wide enough for you. This being a
new section, the planks are a foot or more above the ground. You walk in the road.

In these early Nineties no cash is needed to buy a printing outfit, just an agree-
ment to pay a monthly installment. You buy a Golding press, a type-stand, a small
stone and a few cases of Caslon and an English text. You are probably itching to play
a little with printing. You do not find time to do more than lay the type. A letter
comes from your wife's sister in South Dakota. It states that a neighbor's son or
brother, or some near relative, is in Chicago, that he is interested in art, and it asks
will you look him up. He is a bookkeeper and cashier in a ground-floor real-estate
office at the corner of Clark and Dearborn. His name is Fred Goudy. He wants to get
into the printing business, in a small way. You tell him of your small outfit and that
he can have it and the benefit of payments made if he will assume future install-
ments. He agrees.

THE GAY NINETIES

Chicago a phoenix city risen from the ashes of its great fire; downtown business
buildings, two, three and four stories high, more of former than latter, few a little
higher, elevators a rare luxury; across the river many one-story stores and shops with
signs in large lettering, pioneer style, on their false fronts; streets paved with granite
blocks echo to the rumble of iron-tired wheels and the clank of iron-shod hoofs; a
continuous singing of steel car-cables on State Street and Wabash Avenue; horse-
drawn cross-town cars thickly carpeted with straw in winter; outlying residential
streets paved with cedar blocks; avenues boasting asphalt. Bonneted women with
wasp waists, leg o' mutton sleeves, bustles, their lifted, otherwise dust-collecting,
skirts revealing high-buttoned shoes and gaily-striped stockings; men in brown der-
bies, short jackets, high-buttoned waist-coats, tight trousers without cuffs and, when
pressed, without pleats; shirts with Piccadilly collars and double-ended cuffs of
detachable variety (story told of how a famous author's hero, scion of an old house,
when traveling by train, saw a beautiful young lady, undoubtedly of aristocratic birth,
possibly royal, and wanting to meet her, love at first sight, object matrimony, first
retires, with true blue-blood gentility, to washroom and reverses cuffs. Romance, incident ruthlessly deleted by publisher, proves a best seller). Black walnut furniture
upholstered in haircloth, pride of many a Victorian parlor, is gradually being
replaced by golden oak and ash; painters' studios, especially portrait variety, are hung
with oriental rugs and littered with oriental screens and pottery. High bicycles, the
Columbia with its little wheel behind and the Star with the little wheel in front, soon
to disappear, are still popular. Low wheels, called "safeties," are beginning to appear,
occasionally ridden by women wearing bloomers. Pneumatic tires unknown.

Recognized now as a period of over-ornamentation and bad taste, the Nineties were nevertheless years of leisurely contacts, kindly advice and an appreciative pat on the back by an employer, and certainly a friendly bohemianism seldom known in the rush and drive of today.

Eugene Field has just returned from a vacation in Europe and in his column, *Sharps and Flats*, Chicago is reading the first printing of *Wynken, Blynken and Nod*. Way & Williams, publishers, have an office on the floor below my studio. Irving Way, who would barter his last shirt for a first edition, his last pair of shoes for a volume from the Kelmscott Press of William Morris, is a frequent and always stimulating visitor.

"Will," says Irving, "be over at McClurg's some noon soon, in Millard's rare book department, the 'Amen Corner.' Field will be there, and Francis Wilson, who is appearing at McVickar's in *The Merry Monarch*, and other collectors. Maybe there'll be an opportunity for me to introduce you—and Francis Wilson might ask you to do a poster."

I go to the Press Club occasionally with Nixon Waterman, the columnist who was later to write his oft-quoted, "A rose to the living is more, If graciously given before The slumbering spirit has fled, A rose to the living is more Than sumptuous wreaths to the dead." We sit at table with Opie Read, the well-loved humorist; Ben King, who wrote the delightful lament, "Nothing to eat but food, nowhere to go but out"; Stanley Waterloo, who wrote *The Story of Ab* and, with Luders, the musical comedy, *Prince of Pilsen*, and other newspaper notables whose names I have forgotten.

Two panoramas, *Gettysburg* and *Shiloh*, are bringing welcome wages to landscape and figure painters who will soon migrate to St. Joe across the lake and return in the fall with canvases to be hung at the Art Institute's annual show.

Only one topic on every tongue—the coming World's Fair.

Herbert Stone is at Harvard. He and his classmate, Ingalls Kimball, quickened with enthusiasm and unable to await their graduation, have formed the publishing company of Stone & Kimball. On paper bearing two addresses, Harvard Square, Cambridge, and Caxton Building, Chicago, Herbert commissions a cover, title-page, page decorations and a poster for *When Hearts Are Trumps*, a book of verse by Tom Hall —my first book assignment. This pleasing recognition from a publishing house is followed by a meeting with Harriet Monroe and a Way & Williams commission for a cover and decorations for the *Columbian Ode*.

Your studio is now in the Monadnock building. It is the year of the World's Fair. You have an exhibit that has entitled you to a pass. Jim Corbett is in a show on the Midway. When he is not on the stage you can see him parading on the sidewalks. Buffalo Bill is appearing in a Wild West show. An edition of *Puck* is being printed in one of the exhibition buildings.

You design a cover for a Chicago and Alton Railroad folder. The drawing goes to Rand McNally for engraving and printing. Mr. Martin asks you to come and see him. His salary offer is flattering. But, aside from Bridwell's designs at Mathews Northrup's in Buffalo, railroad printing is in a long-established rut, void of imagination. You prefer free-lancing. Later Mr. Martin buys the K & L plant. Herbert Rogers, the former bookkeeper, establishes his own plant and you hope he will continue the K & L tradition.

Mr. McQuilkin, editor of *The Inland Printer*, commissions a permanent cover. When the design is finished I ask:

"Why not do a series of covers—a change of design with each issue?"

"Can't afford them."

"How about my making an inducement in the way of a tempting price?"

"I'll take the suggestion to Shephard."

Suggestion approved by Henry O. Shephard, printer and publisher, and the series is started—an innovation, the first occasion when a monthly magazine changes its cover design with each issue. One cover, nymph in pool, is later reproduced in London *Studio*. Another, a Christmas cover, has panel of lettering that four American and one German foundry immediately begin to cut as a type. Later the American Type Founders Company, paying for permission, names the face "Bradley."

A poster craze is sweeping the country. Only *signed* copies are desired by collectors and to be shown in exhibitions. Designs by French artists: Toulouse-Lautrec, Chéret, Grasset, etc., some German and a few English, dominate displays. Edward Penfield's *Harper's Monthly* and my *Chap-Book* designs are only American examples at first available.

Will Davis, manager of the Columbia Theater, has just completed the Haymarket, out on West Madison at Halstead. You design and illustrate the opening-night souvenir booklet. This you do for Mr. Kasten, of McClure's. Thus you meet Mr. Davis. He introduces you to Dan Frohman who commissions you to design a twenty-eight sheet stand for his brother, Charles, who is about to open the new Empire Theater in New York. So you design a poster for *The Masqueraders*, by Henry Arthur Jones. This is probably the first *signed* theatrical poster produced by any American lithographer. Then Dan suggests that you visit New York. You do, and meet Charles. Dan takes you to the Players for lunch. There you see show-bills set in Caslon. They influence all of your future work in the field of typography.

We now move to Geneva, Illinois, and I have my studio in a cottage overlooking the beautiful Fox River.

Holiday covers for *Harper's Weekly, Harper's Bazar, Harper's Young People,* later named *Harper's Roundtable*, page decorations for *Vogue*, a series of full-page designs for Sunday editions of *Chicago Tribune*, Herbert Stone's *Chap-Book* article and other favorable publicity—plucking me long before I am ripe, cultivate a lively pair of gypsy heels; and believing myself, perhaps excusably, equal to managing a printing business, editing and publishing an art magazine, designing covers and posters, I return to Boston, then settle in Springfield, start the Wayside Press, and publish *Bradley: His Book.*

SPRINGFIELD: THE WAYSIDE PRESS

Typography, with nothing to its credit following Colonial times, had reached a low ebb during the Victorian period; and by the mid-Nineties type-founders were casting and advertising only novelty faces void of basic design—apparently giving printers what they wanted; while, adding emphasis to bad taste in type faces, compositors were never content to use one series throughout any given piece of display but appeared to be finding joy in mixing as many as possible.

During the Colonial period printers were restricted to Caslon in roman and italic, and an Old English Text. What gave me my love for Caslon and the Old English Text called Caslon Black I do not know. It may have happened in the Ishpeming

print shop where I worked as a boy, or it may have come as a result of some incident or series of incidents that occurred later and are not now remembered. At any rate, for many years I knew nothing about the history of types or the derivation of type design and probably thought of "Caslon" as merely a trade designation of the type-founder, and my early preference for the face may have been merely that of a compositor who found joy in its use—*as I always have.*

One day in 1895, while busy with the establishment of the Wayside Press in Springfield, Massachusetts, I was inspired by some quickening of interest to make a special trip to Boston and visit the Public Library. There I was graciously permitted access to the Barton collection of books printed in New England during the Colonial period; and, thrilled beyond words, I thus gained some knowledge of Caslon's noble ancestry. The books were uncatalogued and stacked in fireproof rooms which were called the "Barton Safes." I was allowed to carry volumes to a nearby gallery above the reference room, where, at conveniently arranged lecterns along an iron balustrade, I examined them at my leisure and was given the outstanding typographic experience of my life.

Such gorgeous title-pages! I gloated over dozens of them, making pencil memoranda of type arrangements and pencil sketches of wood-cut head and tail pieces and initials. Using Caslon roman with italic in a merry intermingling of caps and lower case, occasionally enlivened with a word or a line in Caslon Black, and sometimes embellished with a crude wood-cut decoration depicting a bunch or basket of flowers, and never afraid to use types of large size, the compositors of these masterly title-pages have given us refreshing examples of a typography that literally sparkles with spontaneity and joyousness. Apparently created stick-in-hand at the case, and unbiased by hampering trends and rules, here are honest, direct, attention-compelling examples of type arrangements reflecting the care-free approach of compositors merrily expressing personalities void of the self-consciousness and inhibitions that always tighten up and mar any mere striving for effect.

This Colonial typography, void of beauty-destroying mechanical precision, is the most direct, honest, vigorous and imaginative America has ever known—a sane and inspiring model that was to me a liberal education and undoubtedly the finest influence that could come to me at this time—1895.

I now become a member of the newly formed Arts and Crafts Society of Boston, possibly a charter member, and contribute two or three cases and a few frames of Wayside Press printing to the society's first exhibition in Copley Hall. This showing wins flattering approval from reviewers—laughter from printers who comment: "Bradley must be crazy if he thinks buyers of printing are going to fall for that old-fashioned Caslon type."

At this time the Caslon mats, imported from England, are in possession of one or two branches of the American Type Founders, probably those in New York and Boston, possibly the Dickenson Foundry in Boston. Less than a year after my original receipt of body sizes of Caslon in shelf-faded and fly-specked packages, these foundries cannot keep pace with orders and it is found necessary to take the casting off the slow "steamers" and transfer mats to the main plant in Communipaw, New Jersey, where they can be adapted to fast automatic type-casters. Here additional sizes are cut and a new series, Lining Caslon, is in the works—and, with novelty faces no longer in demand, foundries outside the combine, not possessing mats, are hurrying cutting.

"When the tide is at the lowest, 'tis but nearest to the turn."

That quotation certainly applies to the year 1895 that had started with so little to its credit in the annals of commercial printing and in which we were now witnessing an encouraging aesthetic awakening in the kindred field of publishing. Choice little volumes printed on deckle-edge papers were coming from those young bookmaking enthusiasts—Stone and Kimball in Chicago and Copeland and Day in Boston —and were attracting wide attention and winning well-earned acclaim. Also there were the Kelmscott Press hand-printed books of William Morris, especially his *Chaucer*, set in type of his own design and gorgeously illustrated by Burne-Jones; the Vale Press books, designed by Charles Ricketts and for which he also designed the type; the exotic illustrations by Aubrey Beardsley in John Lane's *Yellow Book*, all coming to us from London. Then there was the excitement occasioned by our own "poster craze," with its accompanying exhibitions giving advertisers and the general public an opportunity to see the gay designs of Chéret and the astounding creations of Lautrec. All these were indicative of a thought-quickening trend due to have a stimulative influence in the then fallow field of commercial printing.

The Wayside Press which I opened in this year of transition was so named for a very real reason. I had worked in Ishpeming and Chicago so as to earn money to take me back to Boston where I hoped to study and become an artist, the profession of my father. I had always thought of printing as being along the wayside to the achieving of my ambition. And I chose a dandelion leaf as my device because the dandelion is a wayside growth.

On the main business street in Springfield there was a new office building called the Phoenix. In two offices on the top floor of the Phoenix Building I had my studio. Back of the office building there was a new loft building on the top floor of which I was establishing my Wayside Press, a corridor connecting it with the top floor of the Phoenix Building and thus making it easily accessible from my studio. It was an ideal location, and with windows on two sides and at the south end insuring an abundance of sunshine, fresh air and light, the workshop was a cheerful spot and one destined to woo me (probably far too often) from my studio and my only definitely established source of income, my designing.

My first Wayside Press printing, before the publication of my magazine, was a Strathmore deckle-edge sample book. Heretofore all Connecticut Valley paper-mill samples, regardless of color, texture or quality of paper, had carried in black ink, usually in the upper corner of each sheet, information as to size and weight. No attempt had been made to stimulate sales by showing the printer how different papers might be used. But one day, just after the Press opened, I had a visitor who changed all that.

I had a bed-ticking apron that had been made for me by my wife, copying the apron I had worn when at the ages of fifteen to seventeen I had served as job printer and foreman of that little print shop in Ishpeming, where I used to proudly stand, type-stick-in-hand, in the street doorway to enjoy a brief chat with my wife-to-be, then a schoolteacher and my sweetheart, as she was on her way to school. Wearing that apron, and at the stone, is how and where Mr. Moses of the Mittineague Paper Company, first of the Strathmore Paper Company units, found me on the occasion of our first meeting.

In my mind's eye I can see Mr. Moses now as he entered from the corridor. He was wearing a navy blue serge suit that emphasized his slight build and made him appear younger than I had expected. I was then twenty-seven and undoubtedly thought of myself as quite grown up, and I marveled that a man seemingly so young should possess the business knowledge necessary to have put him at the head of an even then well-known mill. The contrast of that natty blue-serge with my striped bed-ticking apron should have made me self-conscious. Perhaps it did; but, filled with the youthful enthusiasm and glorious hopes of a dreamer, I probably had thoughts for nothing but my new print shop and publishing. Seeing me unpacking type, my visitor may have thought my time could have been employed more profitably at my drawing-board, as of course it could—though in my then frame of mind it could not have been employed more enjoyably. Displaying samples of his new line, Mr. Moses asked if I would lay out and print a showing for distribution to commercial printers and advertisers.

I explained that the Wayside Press was being established for the printing of *Bradley: His Book*, an art and literary magazine, and for a few booklets and brochures—publications to which I planned to give my personal attention throughout all details of production, and that I had not contemplated undertaking any outside work.

However, after a moment's brief consideration, I became so intrigued with the printing possibilities of these new Strathmore papers, their pleasing colors and tints, together with their being such a perfect, a literally made-to-order, vehicle for Caslon roman and Caslon Black, that I enthusiastically agreed to undertake the commission —a decision for which I shall always feel thankful.

The favorable publicity won by the use of these "old-fashioned" types on Strathmore papers, convinces me that to attain distinction a print shop must possess personality and individuality. At any rate, my continued use of Strathmore papers with appropriate typography and designs aroused such widespread interest among merchants and advertisers and brought so many orders for printing that it soon produced the need for more space. My plant was then moved to a top loft in a new wing that had been added to the Strathmore mill at Mittineague, across the river from Springfield.

Caslon types on Strathmore papers having proved so popular, business was humming. A "Victor" bicycle catalog for the Overman Wheel Company, involving a long run in two colors on Strathmore book and cover papers, and an historically-illustrated catalog for the new "Colonial" flatware pattern of the Towle Silversmiths of Newburyport, for which Strathmore's deckle-edge papers and Caslon types were strikingly appropriate, together with the increased circulation of *Bradley: His Book*, now a much larger format than the original issues, necessitated the addition of another cylinder press, the largest "Century" then being made by the Campbell Press Company; and also the employment of an additional pressman and two additional feeders, and keeping the presses running nights as well as days, often necessitating my remaining at the plant throughout the full twenty-four hours—quite a change from the humble beginnings of the Wayside Press when one "Universal" and two "Gordon" job presses were believed sufficient for the magazine and booklet printing then planned.

In this growth of the commercial printing involving layouts and supervision, together with trying to edit and publish an art magazine, I had waded far beyond my depth. When I was starting my Wayside Press in Springfield a business man had advised: "Learn to creep before you try to walk, and learn to walk before you try to run." I had tried to run before even learning to creep. Mr. Moses gave me what I am now sure was much good business advice—but, alas, I was temperamentally unfitted to listen and learn and, knowing nothing about finances, was eventually overwhelmed and broke under the strain and had to go away for a complete rest. With no one trained to carry on in my absence it was necessary to cease publication of *Bradley: His Book* and in order to insure delivery on time of the catalogs and other commercial printing, forms were lifted from the presses and transferred to the University Press at Cambridge; and the Wayside Press as a unit, including name and goodwill and my own services, soon followed—a hurried and ill-conceived arrangement that eventually proved so mutually unsatisfactory that I faded out of the picture.

This was a heart-breaking decision for me, and one that but for the wisdom of my wife and her rare understanding and nursing could have resulted in a long and serious illness. No printing and publishing business ever started with finer promise and more youthful enthusiasm than did the Wayside Press and the publication of *Bradley: His Book*, that are now just memories.

Among other magazine covers designed during this period there is one for a Christmas number of *Century.* It brings a request for a back-cover design. Both designs are in wood-cut style and require four printings—black and three flat colors. The DeVinne Press, familiar only with process colors, hesitates to do the printing. That issue carries a Will Bradley credit. When John Lane imports sheets of the *Studio*, edits an American supplement and publishes an American edition, I design the covers.

INTERLUDE IN NEW YORK

And now we are in the Gay Nineties, the mid Gay Nineties, when a hair-cloth sofa adorns every parlor and over-decoration is running riot; when our intelligentsia are reading Anthony Hope's *Prisoner of Zenda*, Stanley Weyman's *Gentlemen of France* and George McCutcheon's *Graustark*; when William Morris is printing *Chaucer*, with illustrations by Burne-Jones, and Aubrey Beardsley is providing an ample excuse for the *Yellow Book*; when LeGallienne's *Golden Girl* is brought over here by John Lane and established in a bookshop on lower Fifth Avenue, and Bliss Carman is singing his songs of rare beauty; when the Fifth Avenue Hotel and the nearby Algonquin are flourishing Madison Square hostelries; when Stern's and McCreery are across the street from Putnam's and Eden Musee, and the modern skyscraper is only an architect's vague dream.

Into this glad era a young man steps off a Twenty-third Street horsecar. This young man, now an ambitious designer, printer, editor and publisher, is yourself.

At the age of twenty-seven you are sporting the encouraging beginnings of a mustache, still too thin to permit of twirling at the tips. There is also the brave suggestion of a Vandyke. These embellishments are brown, as is also true of abundant and wavy hair of artistic and poetic length. Your waistcoat is buttoned high, and your soft, white collar is adorned with a five-inch-wide black cravat tied in a flowing bowknot. Your short jacket and tight-fitting pants quite possibly need pressing. A black derby and well-polished shoes complete your distinguished appearance. Many scrubbings have failed to remove all traces of printing ink from beneath and at the base of your finger nails.

You are on your way to Scribner's. A few moments later we find you seated in a leather-upholstered chair in the editorial department of this famous publishing house. You are waiting patiently and hopefully while an editor is penning a note of introduction to Richard Harding Davis, the popular writer of romantic fiction.

Now, the note safely bestowed in your breast pocket, the envelope showing above a liberal display of silk handkerchief and thus plainly in view of passing pedestrians who would doubtless be filled with envy did they but know its contents, you are crossing Madison Square Park on your way to one of the Twenties, where Mr. Davis has his lodging. You reach the house, walk up the steps and rap.

"Is Mr. Davis at home? Why . . . why you are Mr. Davis. I . . . I didn't recognize you at first. Seeing you portrayed in Mr. Gibson's illustrations to some of your romances—"

"And now seeing me in this bathrobe you naturally were a bit confused?"

"Yes, I was."

"I'm not at all surprised."

"Here, Mr. Davis, is a letter, I mean a note introducing me to you."

"How about coming inside while I read the note?"

"That's . . . that's what I was hoping you'd say, Mr. Davis."

And now our favorite romantic author is seated with one leg thrown over the corner of a table. "Of course. Of course," he exclaims, cordially, "I know your posters and your cover designs. And now you are starting a magazine and you would like one of my stories for your first number?"

"Yes, Mr. Davis. That is what I should like."

"Of course I'll write a story for you. I shall be happy to write a story; and I have one in mind that I think will be just the kind you will like for your new magazine."

"Well, Mr. Davis, that's something that's just about as wonderful as anything that could possibly happen to anybody. Only . . . only—"

"Only you are not really started and your magazine hasn't begun to earn money, and so you are wondering—"

"Yes, Mr. Davis—"

"Well, lad," and now Mr. Davis has his arm about your shoulders. "Well, lad, just go home to your Wayside Press print-shop in Springfield and don't do any worrying about payment. Sometime when you are rich and feel like sending me something—why, any amount you happen to send will be quite all right with me— and good luck go with you."

(At this point it should be stated that when a small check goes to Mr. Davis, with an apology for it being just the first installment and that another check will go a month later, the return mail brings a pleasant letter of thanks and an acknowledgment of payment in full.)

And now, as you are recrossing Madison Square Park, your head so high in the clouds that not even the tips of your toes are touching the earth, all the birds in the neighborhood, including the sparrows, have gathered and are singing glad anthems of joy; and all the trees that an hour ago were just in green leaf are now billowed with beautiful flowers.

Well, that is that, and of course you are now sitting pretty. But presently we see you on a Fifth Avenue bus, returning from Fifty-ninth Street where, in a sumptuous Victorian apartment overlooking Central Park you have asked William Dean Howells for a story—and on this incident we will charitably draw the curtain.

Meanwhile *Bradley: His Book* met with kind reception—advance orders for the second number being: Brentano's, New York, six hundred copies, Old Corner Bookstore, Boston, four hundred, etc.; the first issue being out of print except for the supply being held for new subscribers. Pratt, Sixth Avenue, New York, sent check to pay for one hundred subscriptions.

There being no joy in doing today what one did yesterday, or what another did yesterday; and creative design in which there is no joy or laughter being of little worth, a new layout and change of stock were provided for each issue of *Bradley: His Book*; the fifth number started a change of format.

But as a business tycoon Will Bradley was a lamentable failure despite this auspicious start—a story I have already told.

NEW FIELDS

At the turn of the century, after saying a sad farewell to fond hopes and feeling older at thirty-two than is now true at eighty-two, I finally gave up trying to be a publisher and printer. While covers for *Collier's* were bridging an awkward gap Edward Bok appeared on the scene and commissioned the laying-out of an editorial prospectus for the *Ladies' Home Journal*, the printing to be done at the Curtis plant. For this I used a special casting of an old face not then on the market, Mr. Phinney of the Boston branch of ATF telling me it was to be called Wayside. When the prospectus was finished Mr. Bok invited me to his home just outside Philadelphia and there it was arranged that I design eight full pages for the *Journal*—eight full pages of house interiors. These were followed by a series of house designs. Finding it difficult to keep to merely four walls I added dozens of suggestions for individual pieces of furniture—this being the "Mission" period when such designing required no knowledge of periods, only imagination. Then Mr. Bok suggested that I move to Rose Valley, start a shop to make furniture and other forms of handicraft in line with designs shown in my *Journal* drawings; and assume art editorship of *House Beautiful*, which he was considering buying. But having failed in one business venture, there was little excuse to embark on another.

The roman and italic face, used later for *Peter Poodle, Toy Maker to the King*, was now designed for American Type Founders; and while building a home in Concord, adjoining Hawthorne's "Wayside," and working every day in the open, regaining lost health, I wrote the story, *Castle Perilous*—also outdoors. These activities were followed by a request from Mr. Nelson, president of American Type Founders, that I undertake a campaign of type display and publicity for the Foundry, with a promise to cut any decorative or type designs that I might supply, also to purchase as many Miehle presses as might be required for the printing—an invitation to which I replied with an enthusiastic "Yes!"

During this type-display and foundry-publicity period *Castle Perilous*, as a three-part serial, with illustrations made afternoons following mornings spent with American Type Founders at Communipaw, was published in *Collier's*; and in 1907 I became that publication's art editor. Sometime during the intervening years—I can't remember where or when—time was found for designing several *Collier's* covers.

From 1910 to 1915, again with my own studios, I took care of the art editorship of a group of magazines: *Good Housekeeping, Century, Metropolitan* and others, also an assignment from the Batten Advertising Agency and, as recreation, wrote eleven *Tales of Noodleburg* for *St. Nicholas*.

THE MAGAZINE WORLD—AN INTERPOLATION

For easier understanding by you whose magazine memories do not go back to the turn of the century it should be told that we were then carrying a Gibson Girl hangover from the Gay Nineties and were but a few years removed from a time when there were only three standard monthlies: *Harper's, Scribner's,* and *Century;* and seven illustrated weeklies: *Harper's, Frank Leslie's, Harper's Bazar, Police Gazette, Puck, Judge* and the old *Life,*—magazines and weeklies that were seldom given display other than in hotels and railroad depots, where they were shown in competition with the then-popular paper-covered novels.

In the mid-Eighties all monthlies, weeklies, books and booklets were hand-fed, folded, collated and bound; half-tones were in an experimental stage; advertising agencies, if any existed, were not noticeable in Chicago, and advertising of a national character used only quarter-page cover space. But something in the air already quickened imagination, and the Nineties gave us more magazines and better display.

In 1907, magazines were shedding swaddling clothes and getting into rompers; the *Saturday Evening Post* had cast off its pseudo-Benjamin Franklin dress and adopted a live editorial policy that was winning readers and advertising; Edward Bok had ventured a Harrison Fisher head on a *Ladies' Home Journal* cover and won a fifty-thousand gain in newsstand sales, and Robert Collier had built a subscription-book premium into a national weekly.

THE MAGAZINE WORLD—COLLIER'S AND OTHERS

On a Saturday afternoon in 1907, believing myself alone, for the offices and plant had closed at twelve, I was standing at a drafting table making up the Thanksgiving issue of *Collier's* when Mr. Collier entered. He became intrigued with proofs of decorative units being combined for initial-letter and page borders, as had earlier been done with similar material in designing a cover, and asked for some to take home and play with on the morrow. Robert Collier was that kind of a boss—a joy!

Of the Thanksgiving issue Royal Cortissoz wrote: "This week's number has just turned up and I cannot refrain from sending you my congratulations. The cover is bully; it's good decoration, it's appropriate, it's everything that is first rate. The decorations all through are charming. More power to your elbow. It does my heart good to see *Collier's* turning up in such splendid shape." There were other favorable comments—but no noticeable jump in newsstand sales.

My joining *Collier's* staff had been under circumstances quite exceptional, even for that somewhat pioneer period in which the streamlined editorial and publishing efficiency of today was only a vague dream. I had been asked to give the weekly a new typographic layout. When this was ready Mr. Collier suggested that I take the art editorship. He said I would be given his office in the editorial department and he would occupy one in the book department, where he could devote more time to that branch of the business, an arrangement he knew would please his father. I was to carry the title of art editor but in reality would be responsible for make-up and other details that had been demanding too much of his own time.

At the age of twelve I had begun to learn that type display is primarily for the purpose of selling something. In 1889, as a free-lance artist in Chicago, I had discovered that to sell something was also the prime purpose of designs for book and magazine covers and for posters. Later I was to realize that salesmanship possessed the same importance in editorial headings and blurbs. These never-to-be-forgotten lessons, taught by experience and emphasized by the sales results of the publicity campaign I had lately conducted for the American Typefounders Company, would classify that Thanksgiving number as a newsstand disappointment. However, it pleased Robert Collier who, even to hold a guaranteed circulation—when a loss would mean rebates to advertisers—would not permit the use of stories by such popular writers as Robert Chambers and Zane Grey nor the popular illustrations of such artists as Howard Chandler Christy!

My tenure at *Collier's* gave me a new experience. There I always worked under conditions inviting and stimulating imagination, and there I probably unknowingly shattered many a precious editorial precedent.

Collier's had one of the early color presses akin to those used on newspapers. We decided to use this to print illustrations for a monthly "Household Number" carrying extra stories. The editorial back-list showed no fiction suitable for color; the awarding of one thousand dollars a month for the best story, judgment based upon literary merit, had resulted in the purchase of nothing but literary fog. Mr. Collier told Charles Belmont Davis, fiction editor, to order what was necessary. Charley asked me who could write the type of story needed. I said, "Gouverneur Morris." Mr. Morris, then in California, sent a list of titles accompanied by the request: "Ask Will Bradley to take his pick." We chose *The Wife's Coffin*, a pirate tale. During an editorial dinner at his home Robert Collier read a letter from his father, then out of the city, in which P. F. (his father) wrote: "If you continue printing issues like this last our subscription-book salesmen report the weekly will sell itself." Robert said: "Mr. Bradley can make this kind of a number because he knows the people from whom the salesmen obtain subscriptions. I don't, and any similar undertaking by me would be false and a failure."

During this period of art editorship, and following the layout of a booklet, *Seven Steps and a Landing*, for Condé Nast, advertising manager of *Collier's*, a color-spread for Cluett-Peabody, layouts for the subscription-book department, and pieces of printing for Mr. Collier's social activities (also a request from Medill McCormick that I go to Chicago and supply a new typographic make-up for the *Tribune*; a suggestion from Mr. Chichester, president of the Century Company, that if I were ever free he would like to talk with me about taking the art editorship of *Century*; and from Mr. Schweindler, printer of *Cosmopolitan* and other magazines, an expression of the hope that I could be obtained for laying-out a new publication), Robert Collier proposed the building of a pent-house studio on the roof near his father's office where, relieved of much detail, I could give additional thought to all branches of the business. This promised too little excitement, and instead I rented a studio-office on the forty-fifth floor of the then nearly-finished Metropolitan Tower. At this time Condé Nast had just purchased *Vogue*, then a small publication showing few changes from when I had contributed to it in the early Nineties.

In this new environment I handled the art editorship and make-up of *Metropolitan, Century, Success, Pearson's* and the new *National Weekly*, which was given a format like that of present-day weeklies and a make-up that included rules. Caslon was used for all headings except for *Pearson's* which, using a specially-drawn character, were lettered by hand.

Among some discarded *Metropolitan* covers I found one by Stanislaus—the head of a girl wearing a white-and-red-striped toboggan cap against a pea-green background. By substituting the toboggan-cap red for the pea-green background, with the artist's approval, we obtained a poster effect that dominated the newsstands and achieved an immediate sellout.

ENTER MR. HEARST

In the Nineties I had been asked to provide a layout for the Sunday magazine section of Mr. Hearst's New York paper. I could not do this properly except at my Wayside Press. This the typographic union would not permit, but in the years that followed, I enjoyed an intermittent part-time association with Mr. Hearst—working on magazines, papers and motion pictures.

One of these assignments was *Good Housekeeping*. This magazine had been published by the Phelps Company, and had achieved a circulation of 250,000 copies. Additional sales would tax the plant and necessitate more equipment, and the magazine was sold to William Randolph Hearst. I was asked to design a new layout and to take over the art editorship during its formative period. For the new venture Mr. Hearst ordered a Winston Churchill serial—*The Inside of the Cup* if my memory is not at fault. Mr. Tower, the editor brought from Springfield, said this would mean taking out departments and a loss of half the circulation—but the departments came out, the serial went in, Mr. Tower resigned, Mr. Bigelow became editor, and circulation mounted into the millions!

In 1915 Mr. Hearst asked me if I could arrange to give him all of my time and art-supervise production of the motion picture serial, *Patria*, starring Irene Castle. I agreed.

In 1920, after writing, staging and directing *Moongold*, a Pierrot fantasy photographed against black velvet, using properties but no pictorial backgrounds—an independent production launched with a special showing at the Criterion Theater in Times Square, I returned to Mr. Hearst in an art and typographic assignment including magazines, newspapers, motion pictures and a trip to Europe where commissions were placed with Edmund Dulac, Arthur Rackham and Frank Brangwyn. Somewhere along the trail *Spoils*, a drama in verse, and *Launcelot and the Ladies*, a novel, were written—the former printed in *Hearst's International* and the latter destined to carry a Harper & Brothers imprint—but not to become a best seller.

Another Hearst project in the early Twenties was a new format and the creation of a typographic layout for *Hearst's International*. For the layout, the headings of which would have to be different from those provided earlier for *Cosmopolitan*, I designed a set of initial letters, later catalogued by the foundry and called "Vanity." Knowing that Mr. Hearst would want to use portrait heads for covers and that they would all have to be made by a single artist whose style did not permit of confusion with the Harrison Fisher heads used on *Cosmopolitan*, I approached Benda with the suggestion that if he would use one color scheme for both head and background he could probably get the contract. On seeing the first Benda cover Mr. Hearst asked how it happened that this was the only Benda head he ever liked! He was told, and authorized a contract.

These *Hearst International* changes led to my being asked to give thought to strengthening *Cosmopolitan* headings in 1923. The request came on a Monday morning. The issue then in hand closed at Cuneo's in Chicago on the following Friday. Mr. Hearst never urged hurry, but early results were appreciated. Obtaining a current dummy with page proofs, I headed for the ATF composing room at Communipaw, N.J. About half-past four I had personally set, without justification, every heading in the issue—using Caslon in roman and italic in the manner it had been assembled by uninhibited compositors of the Colonial period. That night, at home, I trimmed and mounted proofs in a new dummy. The mixing of roman and italic in radically different sizes and with consideration for desired emphasis, with possibly a 96- or 120-point roman cap starting a 48- or 60-point italic word, resulted just as I had visualized while the type was being set in fragmentary form. No changes were necessary, and every minute of the afternoon had been good fun. Tuesday I left for Chicago; Wednesday was spent at Cuneo's where, using this reprint copy, all headings were set, made-up with text pages, and proved; Thursday the new layouts were enthusiastically approved in New York; Friday, at Cuneo's, *Cosmopolitan's* managing editor closed the forms according to schedule. It had been a grand lark—and within a few weeks that free style of typography began to appear in national advertising.

One morning a request came from Mr. Hearst to use color at every editorial opening in *Hearst's International*—a startling innovation at a time when illustrators were accustomed to drawing or painting only for reproduction in black and white or for an occasional insert in process colors. Closing day on the current dummy was only two weeks away. With the aid of editorial substitutions it was thought we could make the date. Taking a dummy showing possible signature distribution of colors, I made the round of studios to find artists agreeable to the use of one extra color.

After ten days' work I arrived at the Blackstone Hotel in Chicago, where Mr. Hearst was holding conferences. I had an appointment for noon of the next day. Spending the intervening time at Cuneo's, I finished the dummy and appeared for my appointment, asking at the hotel that Mr. Hearst's secretary be informed. The clerk shook his head; orders had been given that no phone calls were to be put through to that floor. The manager was called, I pointed to my brief-case lying on the counter, and said that Mr. Hearst was waiting for its contents. The manager took a chance, made the call, and I was told to go right up.

The conference was in a large room with windowseats overlooking the lake. We sat on one of these seats while the dummy was viewed—page by page—twice. Mr. Hearst was pleased and asked if he might keep the dummy so he could enjoy it at his leisure. I told him the closing date would not permit this. He understood, and saying so in an appreciative manner suggesting a pat on the back, he sent me off to catch the afternoon limited so I could reach New York in the morning. There I was shown a wire evidently written and sent as soon as I had left. It was to Ray Long, editor-in-chief, saying: "Shall be pleased if future numbers are as attractive as the dummy I have just seen." That is the "Chief"—always stimulating and appreciative!

TOWARDS A NEW STYLE

After retiring from the Hearst organization I was recalled and asked to go to Chicago and see if something could not be done to improve the printing of illustrations. A trip to Chicago was not necessary, there being an obvious change long overdue in the New York art departments, and not in the Cuneo printing plant. This fact was reported to Mr. Hathaway, who had relayed the request from Mr. Hearst in California; but Chicago was in the cards and I went. Upon my return a written report, the substance of which had received Mr. Cuneo's approval, was given to Mr. Long. In lay language, briefly expressed, it said: "Illustrators should be cautioned about an overuse of fussy and valueless detail and asked to restrict their compositions to only so

much of the figure or figures, backgrounds and accessories as are required for dramatic story-telling and effective picture-making; requested to forego a full palette when subjects are to be presented in only one or two colors, and to simplify renderings and avoid so many broken tones. Full-page and spread reproductions will then not only solve your press-room worries but create a new and finer type of magazine."

Mr. Long read the report—thoughtfully, I believe—talked with his art editors, and finally decided the suggestions were too radical. But had Mr. Hearst been in New York, and had the report gone to him, his *Cosmopolitan* and *Good Housekeeping* would have led the field in adopting principles of illustration that are now universal.

When asked to provide a new layout for *McClure's* magazine, then a recent purchase by Mr. Hearst, I reveled in an opportunity to apply the suggestions presented in the report. Making photographic enlargements of available illustrations and eliminating all non-essentials I used full pages and spreads and prepared the dummy with a new note in typographic headings. Ray Long looked at it and gasped. "Will," he said, "a magazine like that would outshine and humble *Cosmo*." Mr. Hearst was still in California. Too bad! I had made suggestions of worth and Mr. Hearst, running true to form, would have weighed their values—not for a revived *McClure's*, perhaps, but for his other magazines.

* * * *

And now there is little more to tell, unless you want to listen to the way I enthuse about our present-day illustrators, their delightfully imaginative composition and masterly use of color. They are grand campaigners! God love them and the editorial lads who give them opportunity and encouragement. They are making an old man mighty happy—yes, making him envy their fun while he is relegated to sheer laziness in the siesta sun of California.

Before final retirement I managed to lay out a new *Delineator*, a new Sunday magazine for the *Herald Tribune* (about 1925), and a layout suggested by early New England news-sheets for the *Yale Daily*, and ... well, I guess that's about all. No! Listen. In these last three layouts I continued to use my beloved Caslon!

TODAY IN 1954

Do conditions today give the ambitious young designer and printer the same opportunities I enjoyed back in the late Victorian period? Not the same, of course, but even greater.

While it is true that the Nineties were literally made to order for a boy who had acquired only such training as was to be had in the sparsely equipped print-shop of a weekly newspaper in a pioneer iron-mining town, today is made to order for the ambitious young designer and printer who is availing himself of the training to be had by even the small-town beginner.

Back in my boyhood days a study of such examples of design and printing as now reach even the most remote outposts of the printing industry, would have taught me more than I learned during a year in the art department, so-called, of the publishing house of Rand McNally in Chicago.

The inspiration to be derived from the text and advertising pages of our standard magazines, together with the creative art of school children and the art magazines, quite unknown at the turn of the century, supplies a liberal education teaching the beginner how to appreciate and use the printing and designing advantages of today.

What are these advantages, and why do they open a door to exceptional opportunities not known in the Nineties? First, and perhaps of greatest importance, is the typographic consciousness now prevalent, especially in the advertising and business world, where it is universally recognized that effective typography and design increase sales.

Another advantage is to be found in the significant mechanical advances of the last few years, the significance of the growing importance of offset printing, presenting so many opportunities yet to be grasped by the designer. And, an infant industry now, but one of vast possibilities, is commercial silk-screen printing.

But upon my return to New York after many years in California I think my greatest thrill came when I witnessed the mechanical setting of type by photography. Always I have liked the feel of putting type into the stick, and I liked to see the composition growing on the galley. In all my years of working with type I have never made a preparatory layout, except when the composition had to be done by another, which happened only on magazine headings after a style had been determined in advance.

But this is an age of layouts, and in this new photographic process with the use of photographic enlargements, there are possibilities for display composition of any required size, and great variety, presenting intriguing possibilities for the creative designer and typographer.

All such steadily growing advances present opportunities which were non-existent back in my own youthful days. Together with the superior training enjoyed by the youth of today, they have changed conditions into a new world fraught with wonderful opportunities far beyond any I knew in the Nineties.

w b

Short Hills, New Jersey
May, 1954

List of Plates

Full-Color Plates

These color plates follow plate 26

Full-Page Plates

[The front cover of the Dover edition is adapted from a Victor Bicycle poster, Overman Wheel Company, Boston, New York   January 1899]

WILL BRADLEY
His Graphic Art

1   Book cover   *c.* 1893

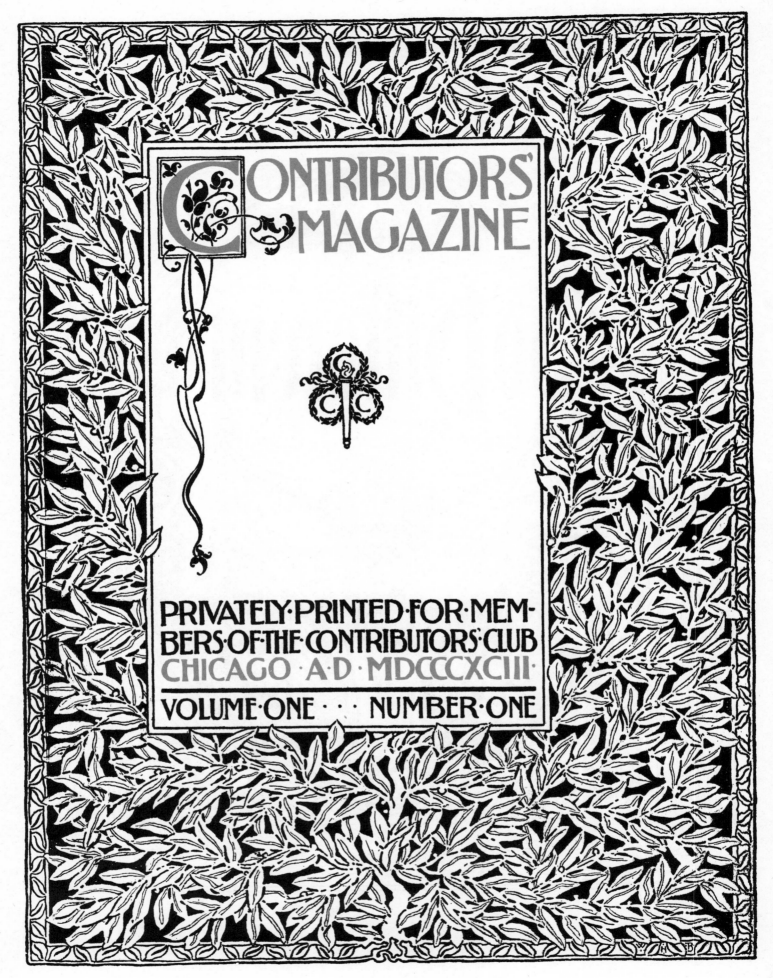

CONTRIBUTORS' MAGAZINE

PRIVATELY·PRINTED·FOR·MEM-
BERS·OF·THE·CONTRIBUTORS'·CLUB
CHICAGO·A·D·MDCCCXCIII
VOLUME·ONE · · · NUMBER·ONE

2   Cover design   1893

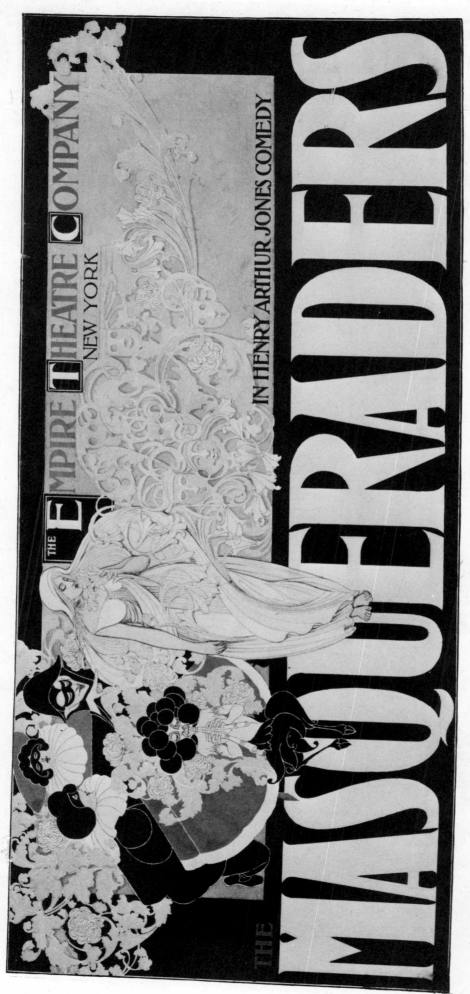

3   Drawing, theatre poster   1894

The Metropolitan Museum of Art, Gift of Fern Bradley Dufner, 1952

THE·INLAND·PRINTER·

4   Cover design   July 1894

5 (*left*) The Skirt Dancer; (*right*) The Serpentine Dancer 1894

6　Illustration, *Chicago Sunday Tribune*　1894

7   Book cover   1894

THE·INLAND·PRINTER
THANKSGIVING·NUMBER·VOL·XIV·NO·2·1894

·Bradley·

8   Cover design   November 1894

9 Poster: The Blue Lady 1894

WILL H BRADLEY

10   The Masquerade   January 1895

Columbia
Bicycles
Pope Manufacturing Co
Hartford Conn. 1895

11   Booklet cover   1895

THE·INLAND·PRINTER

WILL BRADLEY

13   The Dolorous Knight   March 1895

14   Rabboni   April 1895

THE ECHO

CHICAGO'S NEW PAPER · ·
IN WHICH WILL APPEAR A SERIES
OF COLORED FRONTISPIECES BY

WILL H. BRADLEY

FORTNIGHTLY   HUMOROUS AND
ARTISTIC · · ·

WILL H. BRADLEY.

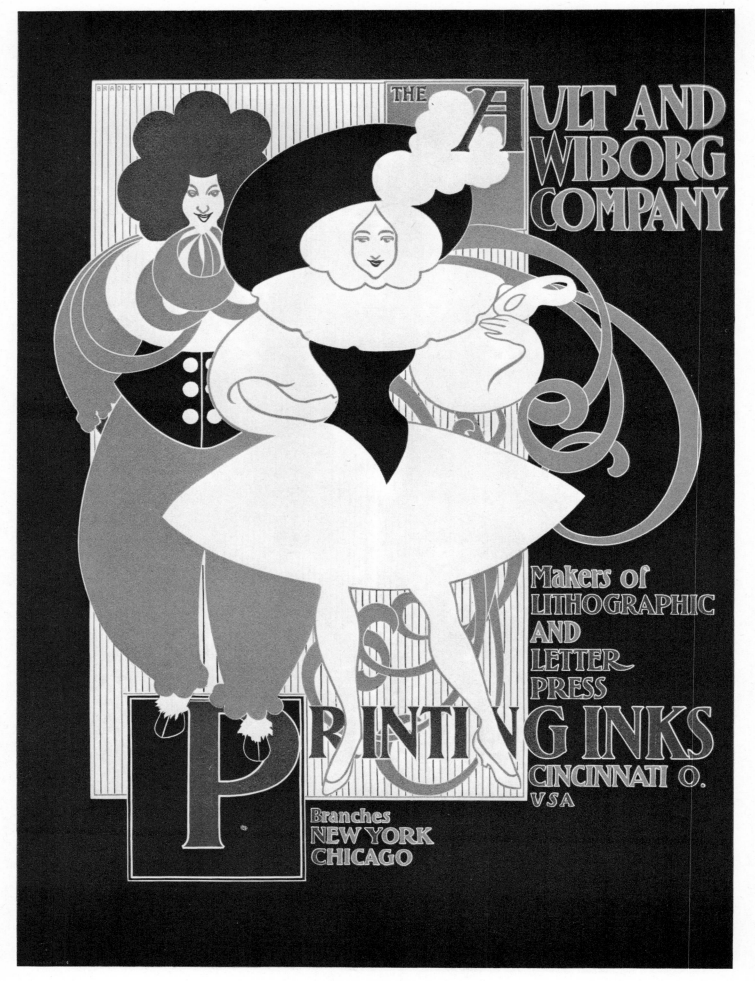

16 Advertisement 1895

17   Frontispiece, title page   1895

18   Eve and the Serpent (*Fringilla*)   1895

19   Pausias and Glycera (*Fringilla*)   1895

20   Poster: The Poet and His Lady   1895

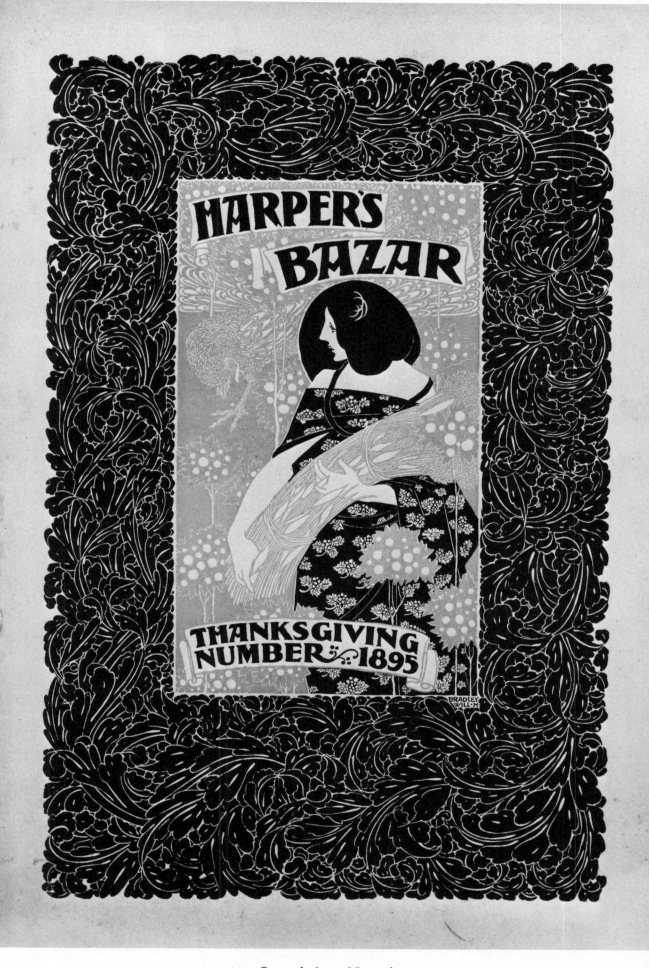

21 Cover design November 1895

22   Poster   1895

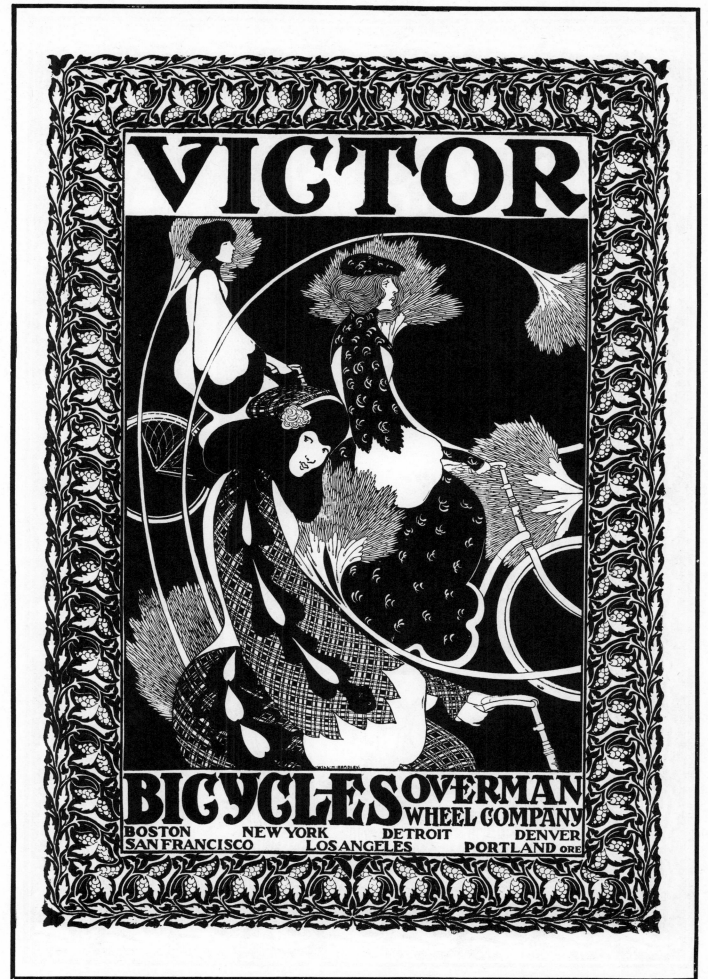

23   Advertisement   December 1895

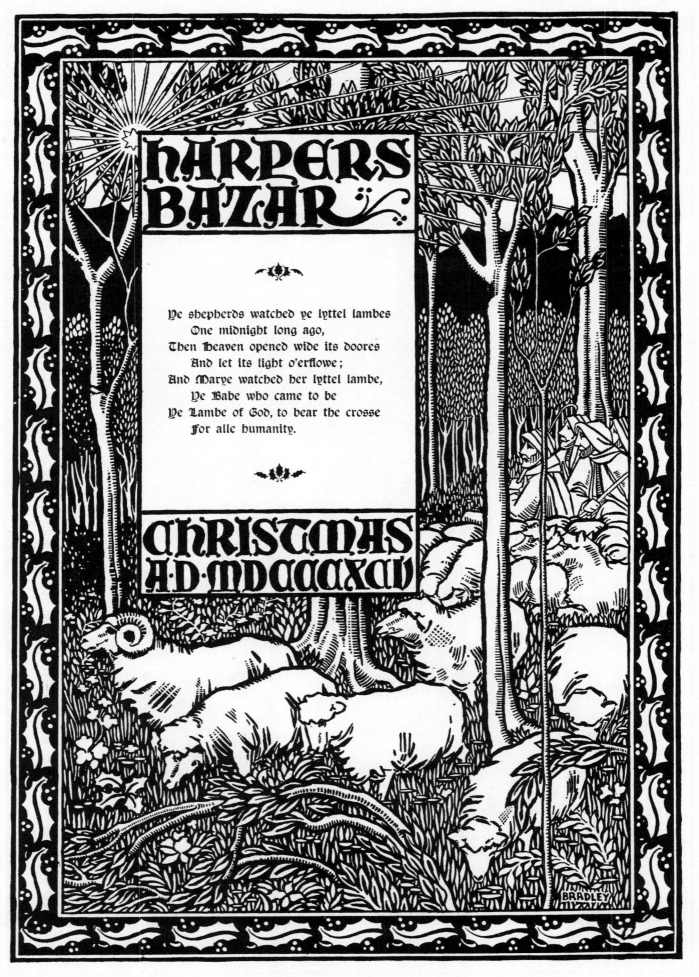

HARPERS BAZAR

Ye shepherds watched ye lyttel lambes
One midnight long ago,
Then Heaven opened wide its doores
And let its light o'erflowe;
And Marye watched her lyttel lambe,
Ye Babe who came to be
Ye Lambe of God, to bear the crosse
For alle humanity.

CHRISTMAS A·D·MDCCCXCV

24 Cover design December 1895

25   Advertisement   April 1896

I Poster: The Twins 1894

WHEN HEARTS
ARE TRUMPS ♥
BY TOM HALL

III   Cover design   December 1895

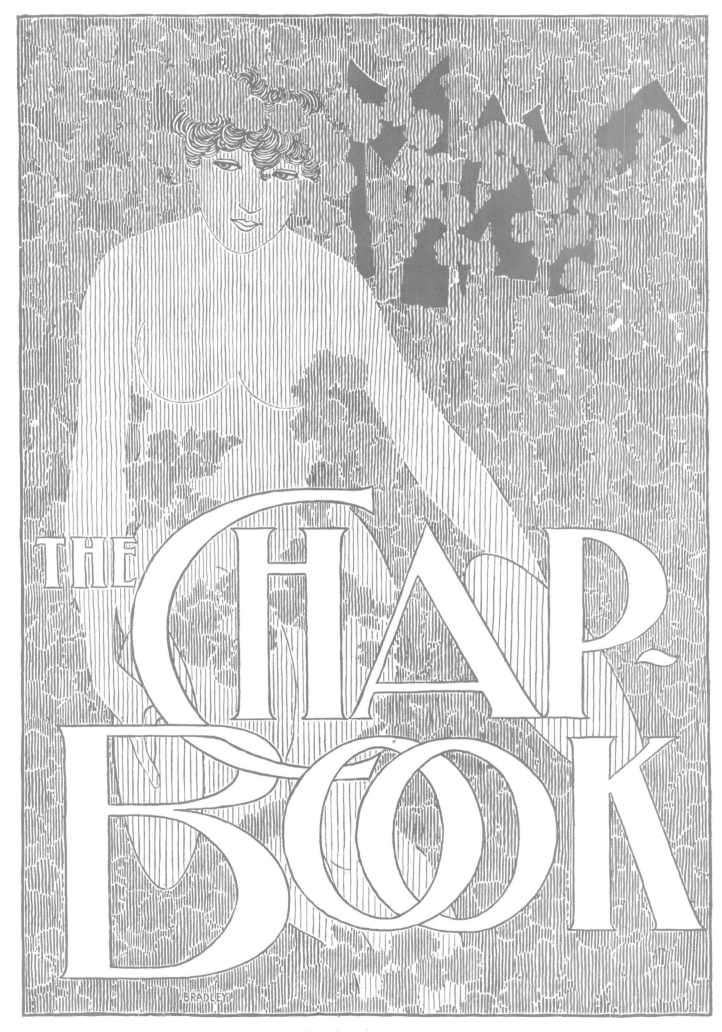

IV   Poster: May   1895

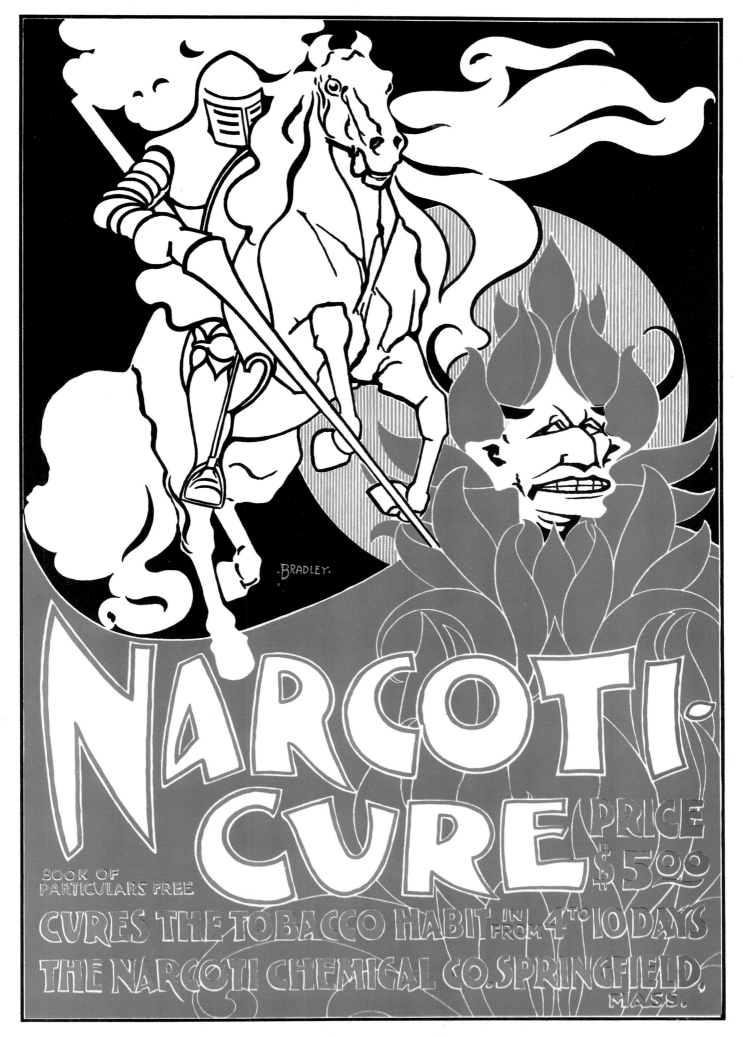

V   Advertisement   1895

VI Advertisement *c*. 1900

VII   Advertisement   *c.* 1900

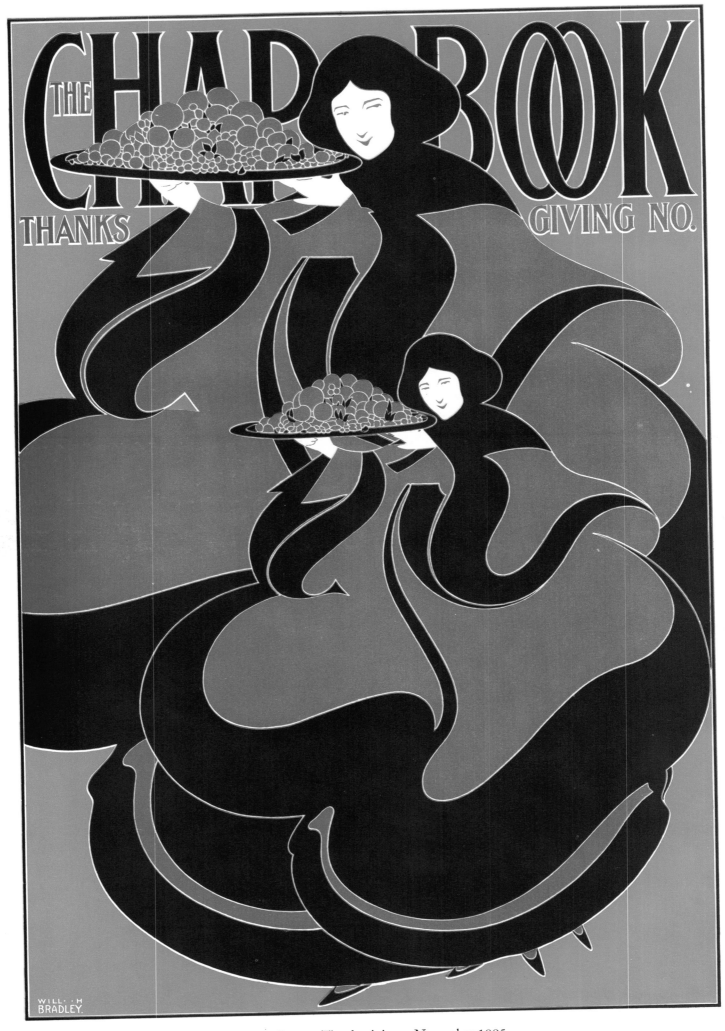

VIII   Poster: Thanksgiving   November 1895

27   Prospectus cover   May 1896

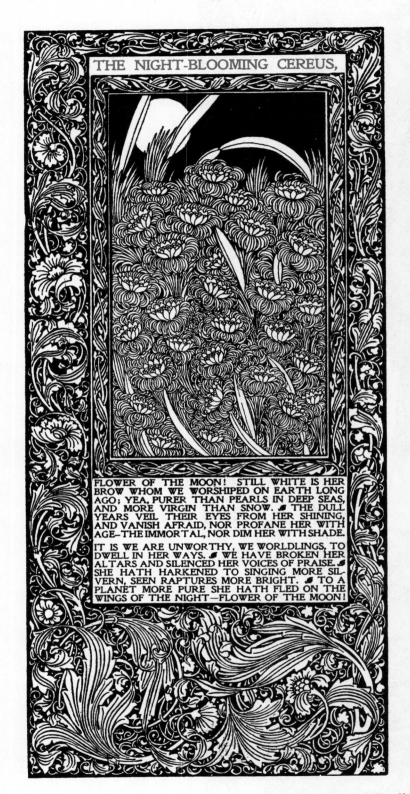

THE NIGHT-BLOOMING CEREUS,

FLOWER OF THE MOON! STILL WHITE IS HER
BROW WHOM WE WORSHIPED ON EARTH LONG
AGO; YEA, PURER THAN PEARLS IN DEEP SEAS,
AND MORE VIRGIN THAN SNOW. ✒ THE DULL
YEARS VEIL THEIR EYES FROM HER SHINING,
AND VANISH AFRAID, NOR PROFANE HER WITH
AGE—THE IMMORTAL, NOR DIM HER WITH SHADE.

IT IS WE ARE UNWORTHY, WE WORLDLINGS, TO
DWELL IN HER WAYS. ✒ WE HAVE BROKEN HER
ALTARS AND SILENCED HER VOICES OF PRAISE. ✒
SHE HATH HARKENED TO SINGING MORE SIL-
VERN, SEEN RAPTURES MORE BRIGHT. 🍃 TO A
PLANET MORE PURE SHE HATH FLED ON THE
WINGS OF THE NIGHT—FLOWER OF THE MOON!

A POEM, BY HARRIET MONROE.

YET SHE LOVETH THE WORLD THAT FORSOOK
HER, FOR LO! ONCE A YEAR, SHE, DIANA, TRANS-
LUCENT, PALE, SCINTILLANT, DOWN FROM HER
SPHERE FLOATETH EARTHWARD LIKE STAR-
LADEN MUSIC TO BLOOM IN A FLOWER; AND OUR
SOULS FEEL THE SPELL OF THE GODDESS, ONCE
MORE, FOR AN HOUR.

SEE! SHE SITTETH IN SPLENDOR NOR KNOWETH
DESIRE NOR DECAY; AND THE NIGHT IS A GLORY
AROUND HER MORE BRIGHT THAN THE DAY. ✒
AND HER BREATH HATH THE SWEETNESS OF
WORLDS WHERE NO SORROW IS KNOWN, AND WE
LONG AS WE WORSHIP TO FOLLOW HER BACK
TO HER OWN—FLOWER OF THE MOON!

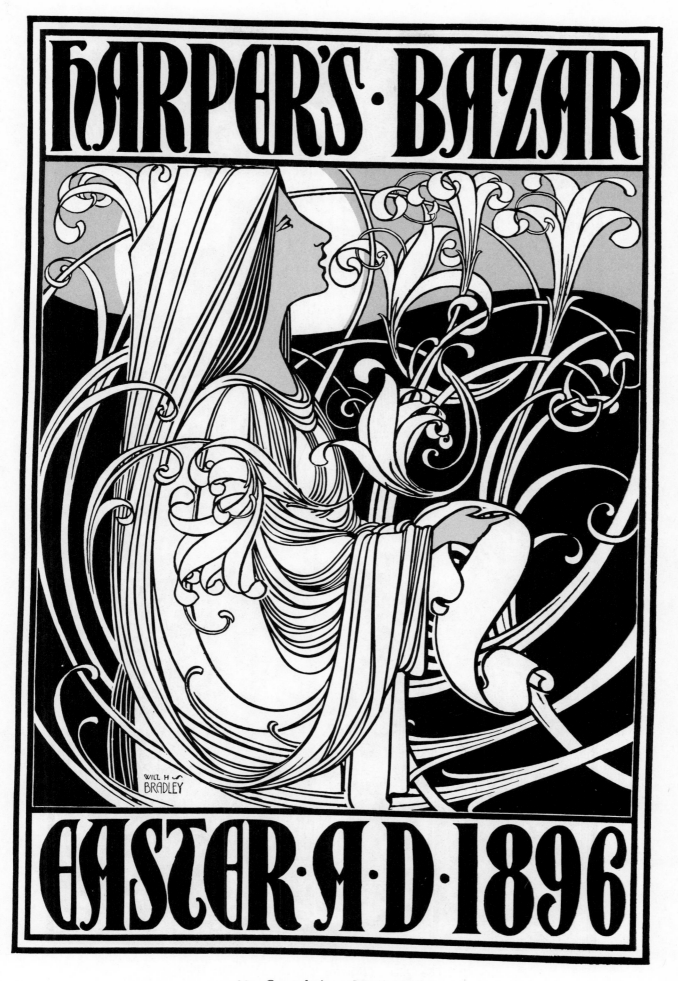

29 Cover design March 1896

30   The Queen (*Bradley: His Book*)   June 1896

Bradley His Book

For July, the same being daintily print
ed and titled a WOMANS NUMBER
For sale by book venders at 25 cents.
Published by the Wayside Press at
the Sign of the Dandelion on the
Town Street Springfield.Mass.USA

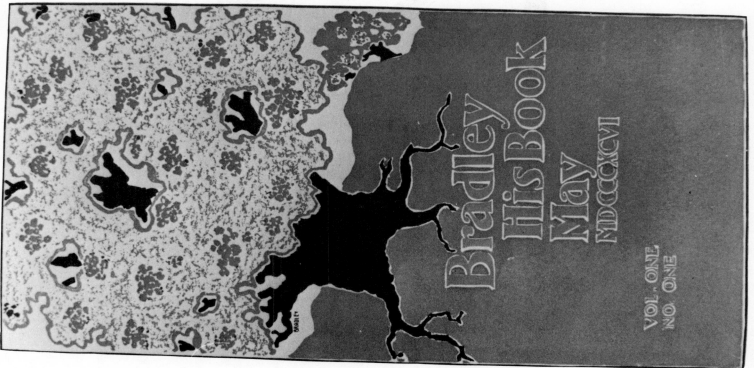

Bradley
His Book
May
MDCCCXCVI

VOL. ONE
NO. ONE

31 Designs, *Bradley: His Book* 1896

32   Illustration, *Bradley: His Book*   June 1896

34 Mary 1896

Christmas Number of The Inland Printer A Technical Journal Devoted to the Art of Printing Published at 212 & 214 Monroe Street Chicago USA Volume XIV Number III A Eighteen Hundred & Ninety Four

35   Cover design   December 1894

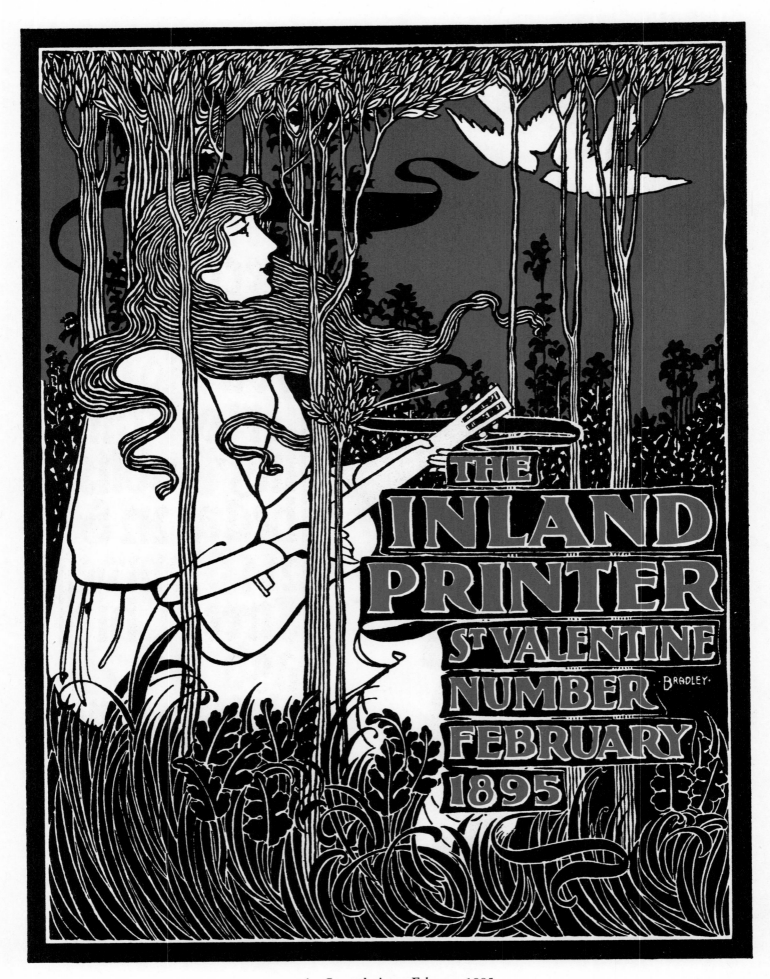

36   Cover design   February 1895

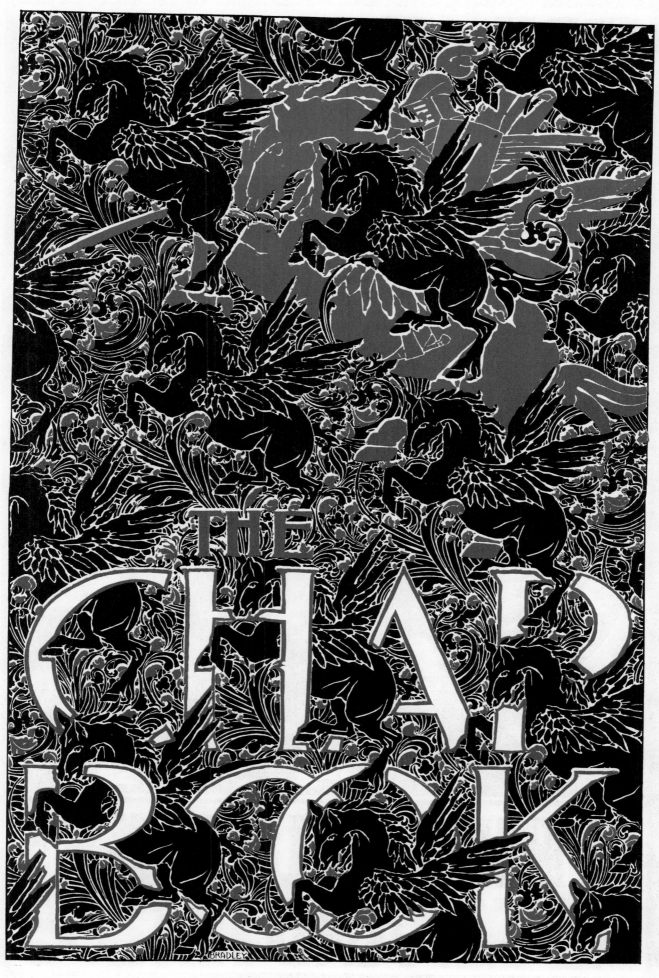

37   Poster: Pegasus   September 1895

39 Cover design November 1895

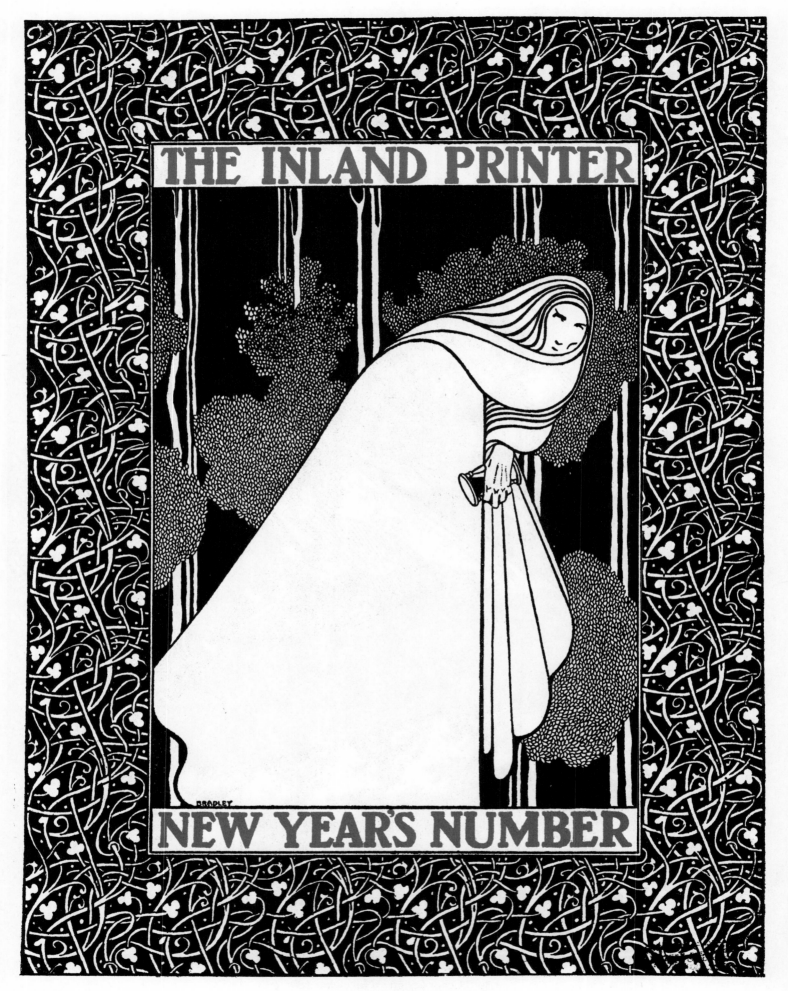

40   Cover design   January 1896

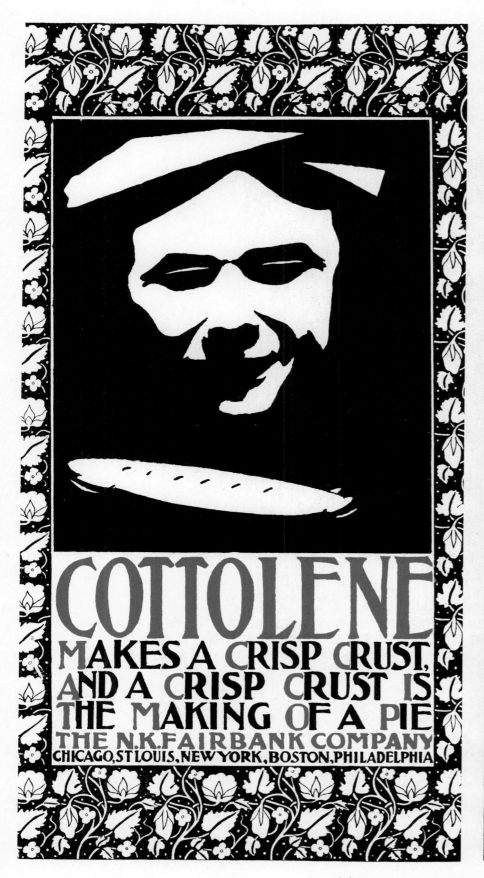

COTTOLENE MAKES A CRISP CRUST, AND A CRISP CRUST IS THE MAKING OF A PIE
THE N.K.FAIRBANK COMPANY
CHICAGO, ST.LOUIS, NEW YORK, BOSTON, PHILADELPHIA

WHITING'S PAPERS.

THE WITCH FOLDEROL GOES FORTH TO MEET THE YOUNG PRINCE JUNEBUG.

42   Design, *Bradley: His Book*   December 1896

43   They Were Both Shaggy Toys   July 1896

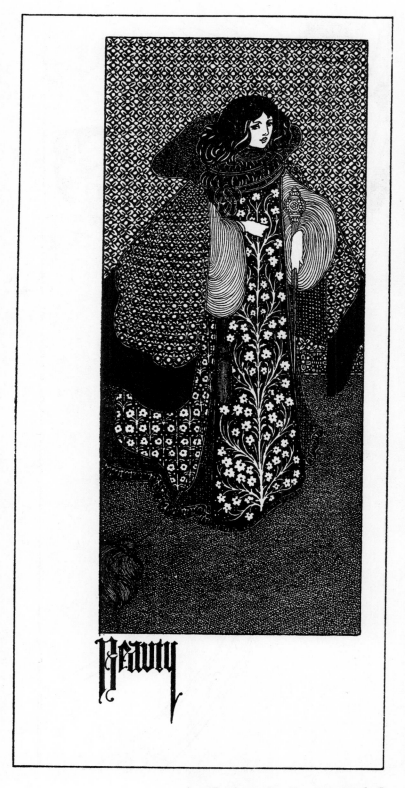

45   Designs, *Bradley: His Book*: Beauty and the Beast   August 1896

46–47   Selected pages, Beauty and the Beast   August 1896

49   The Kiss (*Bradley: His Book*)   November 1896

50   Design, *Bradley: His Book*   November 1896

51 Advertisement February 1896

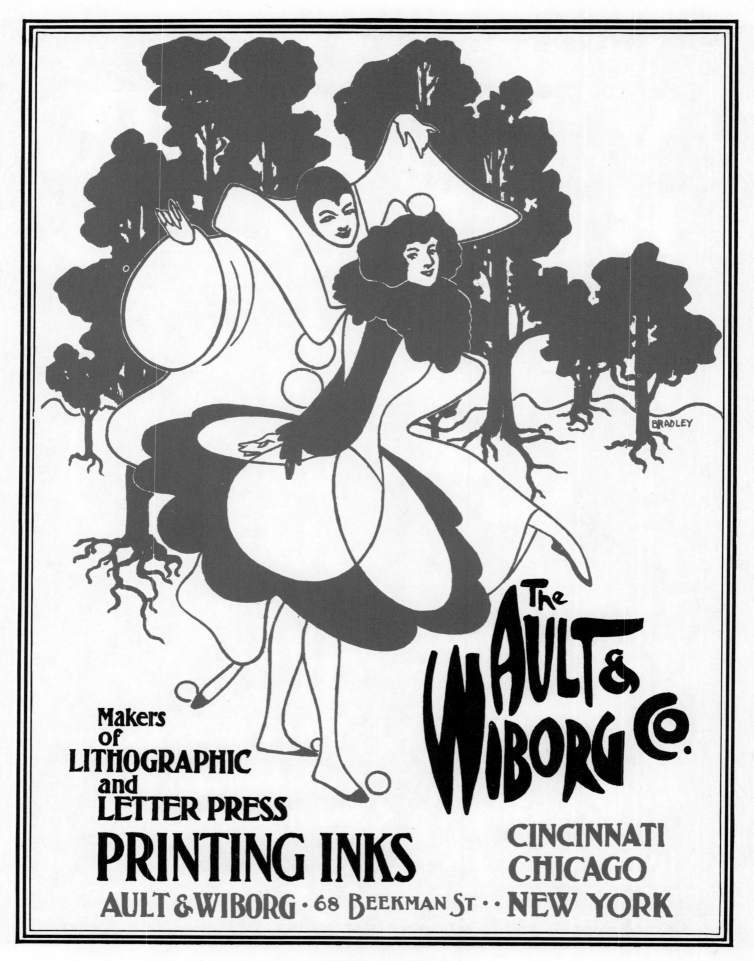

53 Advertisement 1897

Jackson Typewriter

54   Advertisement   1899

55 Advertisement *c.* 1900

A

JAMES BOYNTON

BOARDING AND
SALE STABLE

MAPLE STREET

C

Our business is Fine Printing.
If you are planning a catalogue,
booklet, announcement, circular
or any matter designed to pro-
mote your business, our services
will be of value to you. Samples
and estimates furnished on any
work worthy of special attention

Browne & Markson

Engravers and Printers

No. 3152 Columbia Avenue, Brighton

D

SURPRISED?

*Well, so is everybody when
they see the big bargains we
have to offer. Our stock was
never so large as at present,
and it embraces everything
of the very best kind from a
tin dipper to a cooking stove.*
CASH HARDWARE CO.

B

A *Dissertation* UPON ROAST PIG By Charles Lamb

57   Bradley gift book   *c.* 1902

58   Design, *Peter Poodle*   1906

The INTERNATIONAL STVDIO

An Illustrated Monthly Magazine of FINE & APPLIED ART Edited by CHARLES HOLME Published by JOHN LANE The Bodley Head at 140 Fifth Ave New York Price 35 cents Yearly Subscription $3.50 post paid

59   Cover design   June 1897

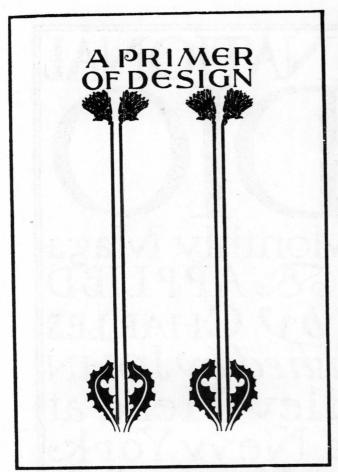

60–61 Facing pages, *Bradley: His Book: (left)* Simple Sprig Patterns;
(right) Repeating Patterns   January 1897

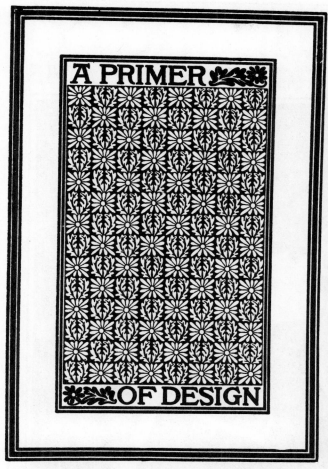

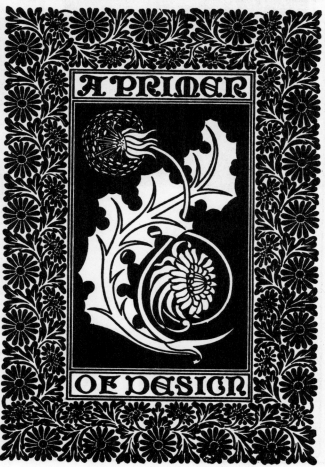

THE AVLT & WIBORG CO
CINCINNATI, NEW YORK, CHICAGO, ST. LOVIS

MF'R'S OF LITHOCRAPHIC and LETTER PRESS
PRINTING INKS

62   Advertisement   *c.* 1897

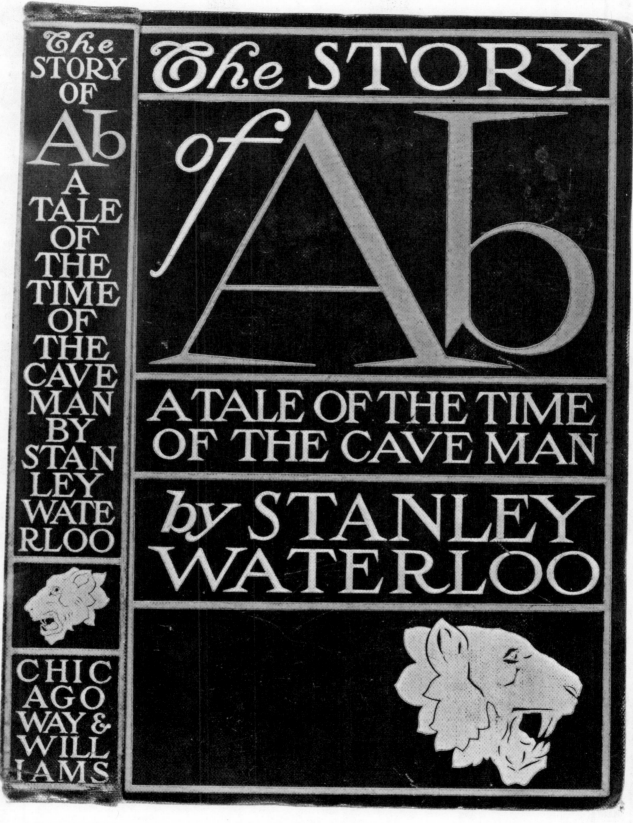

63   Book cover   1897

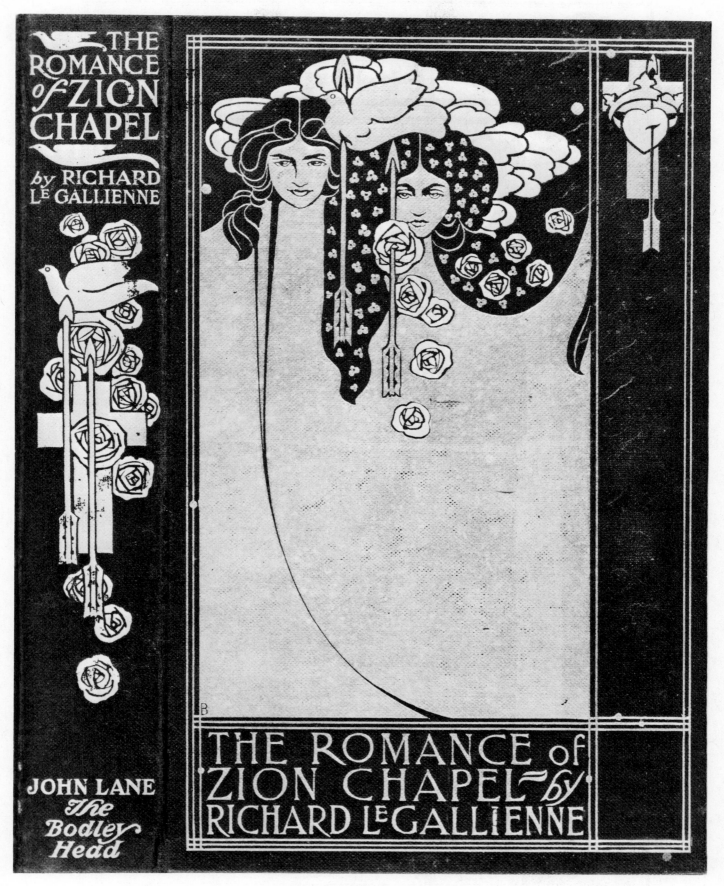

65   Book cover   1898

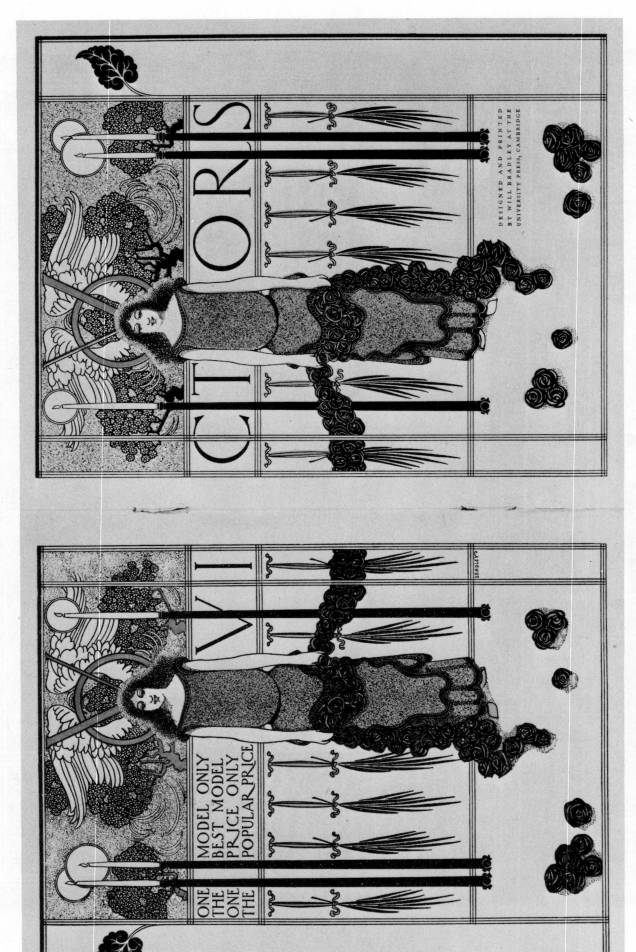

66 Victor Bicycle catalogue 1899

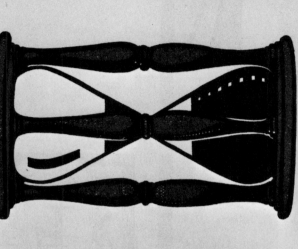

ABOVT MEN
MDCCCXCIX

NEW YORK
ROGERS, PEET
& COMPANY
OUTFITTERS

1800

67   Advertising booklet   1899

68   Booklet title pages   *c.* 1899

Printing

MDCCCXCIX

69   Cover design   1899

70   Cover design   December 1899

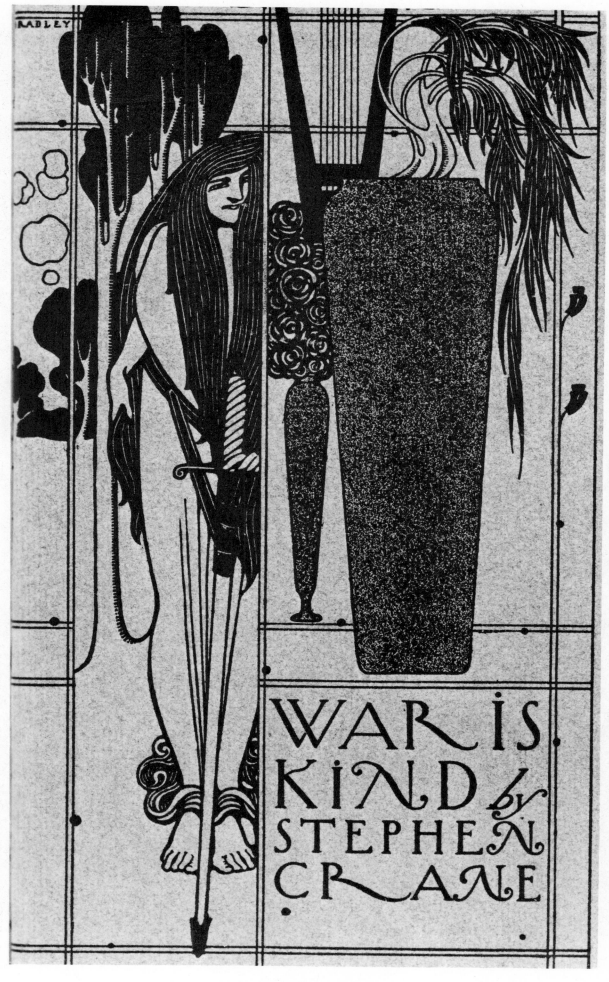

71   Book cover   1899

72   Cover design   July 1900

73 Advertisement 1900

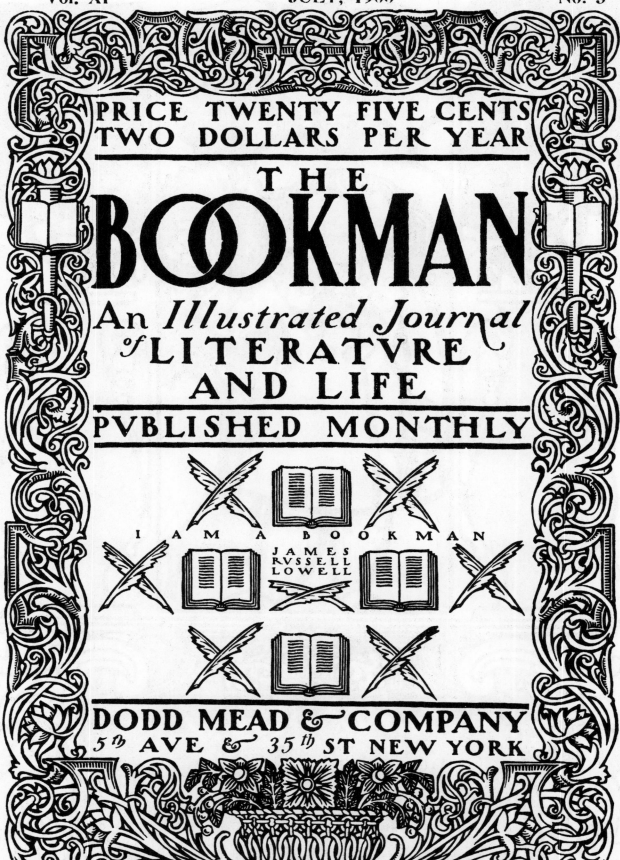

Vol. XI   JULY, 1900   No. 5

PRICE TWENTY FIVE CENTS
TWO DOLLARS PER YEAR

THE

BOOKMAN

An *Illustrated Journal*
of LITERATURE
AND LIFE

PVBLISHED MONTHLY

I AM A BOOKMAN

JAMES
RVSSELL
LOWELL

DODD MEAD & COMPANY
5th AVE & 35th ST NEW YORK

74   Cover design   1900

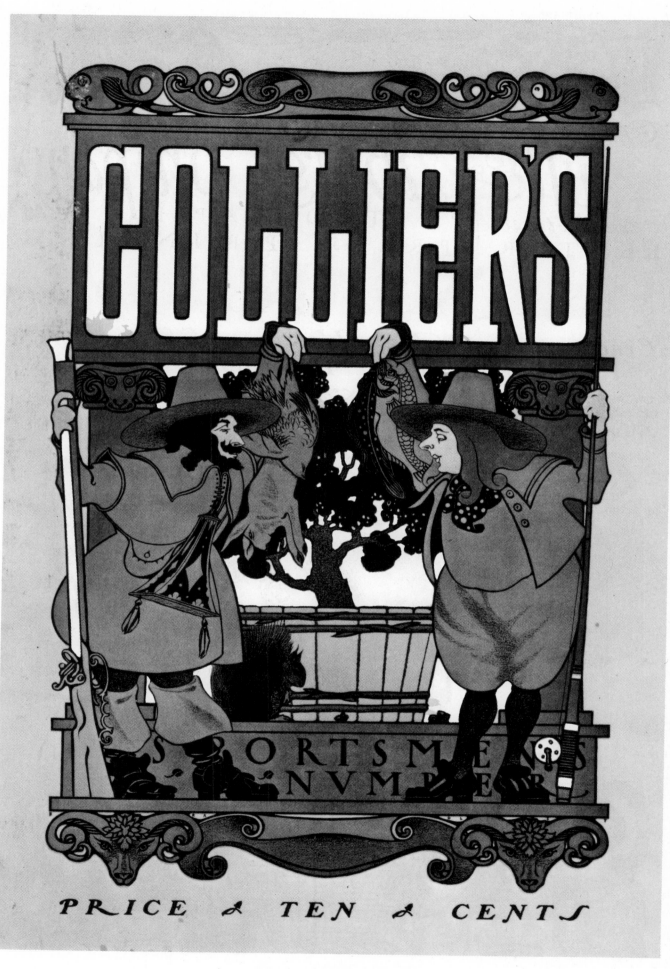

75   Cover design   1900

The Ault & Wiborg Company

Manufacturers of LITHOGRAPHIC & LETTER PRESS PRINTING INKS

Cincinnati   New York   Chicago
St Louis   London

76   Advertisement   c. 1900

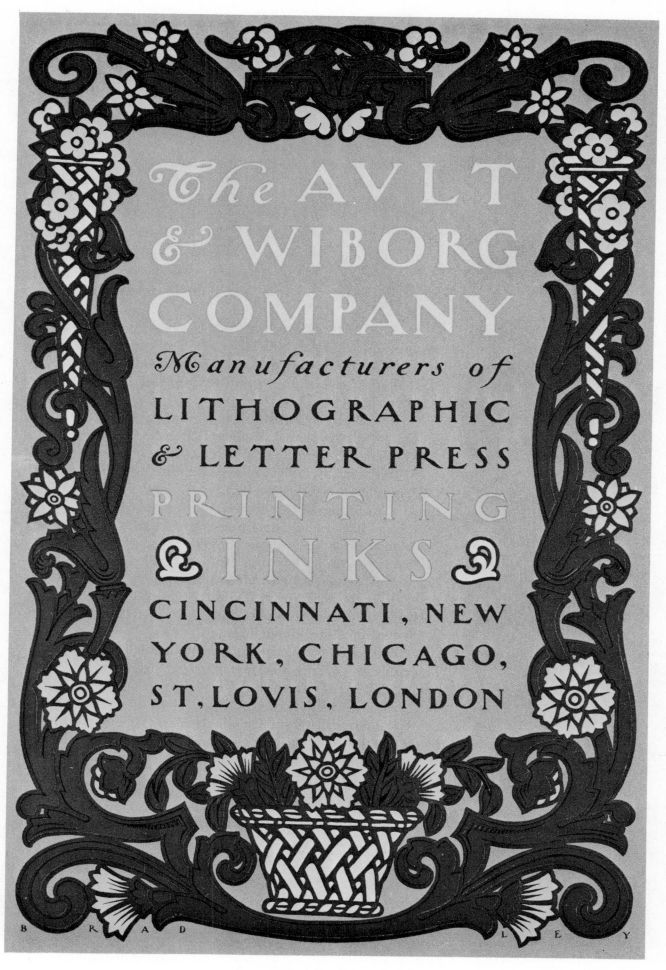

77   Advertisement *c.* 1900

78   Design for a living room   1901

79 Design for a hall 1901

80   Advertisement   *c.* 1900

81   Drawing for *Collier's* cover   November 1901

83   Illustration, *Shards of the Silver Sword*   c. 1902

Book of **CHAP-BOOK** *CUTS*

The PRINTER MAN'S JOY, Being The

& BORDERS, With Sundry Goodly TYPES

AMERICAN *Type Founders Co.*

84   Cover design   1905

85   Frontispiece, *Peter Poodle*   1906

Colliers

THE NATIONAL WEEKLY

Knight
The
Errant

DECEMBER 21 1907   VOL XL NO 13   PRICE 10 CENTS $5.20 A YEAR

86   Cover design, The Knight Errant   December 1907

87   Cover of Will Bradley issue   1913

88   Illustration, *The Wonderbox Stories*   1916

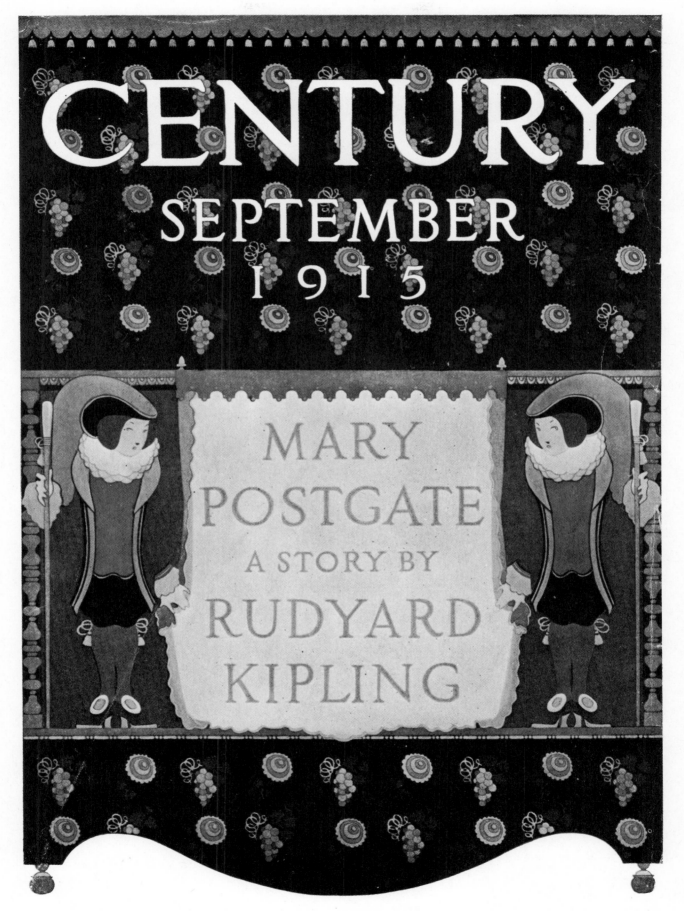

89   Cover design   1915

DATE DUE